Faithful Disagreement

Faithful Disagreement

*Wrestling with Scripture
in the Midst of Church Conflict*

FRANCES TAYLOR GENCH

WESTMINSTER
JOHN KNOX PRESS
LOUISVILLE · KENTUCKY

First edition
Westminster John Knox Press
Louisville, Kentucky

09 10 11 12 13 14 15 16 17 18—10 9 8 7 6 5 4 3 2 1

Book design by Drew Stevens
Cover design by Jennifer K. Cox
Cover art courtesy of La Fleur Studio, © Images.com/Corbis

Library of Congress Cataloging-in-Publication Data

Gench, Frances Taylor, 1956–
  Faithful disagreement : wrestling with Scripture in the midst of church conflict / Frances Taylor Gench.—1st ed.
      p. cm.
  Includes indexes.
  ISBN 978-0-664-23338-9 (alk. paper)
  1. Church controversies—Biblical teaching.   2. Bible—Criticism, interpretation, etc.
  I. Title.
  BV652.9.G46   2009
  250—dc22
                                                        2008039361

With Gratitude

Mark Achtemeier
Scott D. Anderson
Barbara Everitt Bryant
Milton J Coalter
Victoria G. Curtiss
Gary W. Demarest
Jack Haberer
William Stacy Johnson
Mary Ellen Lawson
Jong Hyeong Lee
John B. (Mike) Loudon
Joan Kelley Merritt
Lonnie J. Oliver
Martha D. Sadongei
Sarah Grace Sanderson-Doughty
Jean S. (Jenny) Stoner
José Luis Torres-Milán
Barbara G. Wheeler
John Wilkinson

Gradye Parsons
Bobbie Montgomery
Sharon Youngs

Contents

Introduction

Church conflicts are always "family feuds," for believers—like it or not—are bound to each other by baptism as brothers and sisters in Jesus Christ. And family feuds beget a peculiar pain and intensity. My hope for this book is that it might foster conversation in the midst of church conflict—conversation with both the Bible and fellow Christians with whom we disagree. While it grows out of my own engagement with ecclesial conflict in a particular denomination, the Presbyterian Church (U.S.A.), Presbyterians are hardly the only Christians absorbed in family feuds at present. Thus I hope the studies presented here can be a resource for reflection in other conflicted churches as well. Conflict is a perennial reality in the life of the Christian community, and whatever its focus or setting (congregational or denominational), the Bible can help us live more faithfully with our disagreements and more fully into the peace, unity, and purity that is God's gift to us in Jesus Christ.

But there is a catch: this requires that we read it. The Bible, to be sure, features prominently in most ecclesial family feuds, given our reverence for it. All parties to a church conflict typically invoke it to justify their own positions. Indeed, many of us are quite accomplished at arguing *about* the Bible. But ironically, as theologian John Burgess tellingly observes, "Presbyterians are better at asserting the authority of Scripture than at actually opening the Bible"—and I suspect the same holds true for more than a few Lutherans, Methodists, and Episcopalians (not to mention others). As Burgess notes, "The church's appeal to biblical authority is more often rhetorical than real. Our arguments about Scripture frequently expose just how little we really know the Bible itself. We appeal to a select handful of passages to justify our positions but lack the capacity to order Scripture as a whole. We say that the Bible matters but spend remarkably little time actually reading it."[1] What is needed? Burgess insists that "the church desperately needs to recover practical disciplines of reading Scripture as a Word of God. We do not simply need a better method of interpretation; we need a piety, a different set of dispositions and attitudes toward Scripture. We need a reverent confidence that these words set forth a Word of God for us. . . . We cannot simply wait for the church to get its act together; we must begin now to rediscover the power of Scripture to remold us as a community of faith."[2]

The point I wish to underscore is that we need not only to read the Bible, but to do so in the company of others—especially in the company of those with whom we disagree. What if we were to stop shaking it at each other, actually open it, and read it together? The challenge would be learning to listen—to both the Bible and each other. Learning to listen to the Bible is an ongoing challenge throughout our lives, for as Karl Barth once warned, "the Bible does not always answer our questions, but sometimes calls our questions into question."[3] But listening to the Bible in the midst of church conflict presents its own difficulties. Raymond E. Brown wisely put his finger on the problem when he said, "I contend that in a divided Christianity, instead of reading the Bible to assure ourselves that we are right, we would do better to read it to discover where we have not been listening."[4] For this we need the company of others, especially our "adversaries"; but learning to listen to them—even sitting down with them!—is every bit as difficult, given our tendency to deny that those we disagree with have anything to teach us.

The studies in this book grew out of a profoundly challenging learning experience in the art of listening in which I was engaged over the course of five years (2001–2006), and a few words about that experience are needed, as it is referenced at several points in the chapters that follow. In 2001 the 213th General Assembly of the Presbyterian Church (U.S.A.) decided that our deeply conflicted denomination needed a theological task force to wrestle with the issues uniting and dividing us as Presbyterians, praying that with the help of the Holy Spirit we might lead the church in discernment of our Christian identity and of ways that our church might move forward, furthering its peace, unity, and purity. Three of its moderators—Jack Rogers (2001), Syngman Rhee (2000), and Freda Gardner (1999)—were directed to appoint members. So in their infinite wisdom, these three former moderators collared twenty Presbyterians as different from one another as they could possibly be—twenty Presbyterians who under ordinary circumstances never would have dreamed of hanging out together! So much of the diversity within the PC(USA) was reflected on our task force that when he first met with us, Stated Clerk Cliff Kirkpatrick told us that his office had received no complaints about the makeup of the task force, but had been asked repeatedly, "*How* will they ever get along?" Most of us were wondering the same thing when we first got together. I for one was not at all sure that I wanted to be drafted. But friends and comrades in the pitched battles in which we found ourselves engaged exhorted me to take it on, to get in there and "speak the truth." So I put on the whole armor of God and flew to Dallas ready to knock heads and "speak the truth." This was going to be my opportunity to set some very misguided Presbyterians straight.

Over the course of our five years together, we task force members received a great deal of mail, representing the entire spectrum of opinion in our church—much of it exhorting us to "speak the truth"—a lot of that exhortation accompanied by biblical quotation and commentary and threats of hell and eternal damnation. Indeed, one of the most important things I learned from the whole experience was that we have all been so busy "speaking the truth" to each other that nobody has been listening! We aren't actually having a conversation! *We've* all got truth by the short hairs, *everyone else* is in denial, and we have to set them straight. I came to recognize an important form that denial often takes in my own life, perhaps in yours as well: the denial that people I disagree with have anything to teach me.

It was a hard lesson to learn, but one for which I am grateful and for which I have twenty diverse Presbyterians, to whom this book is dedicated, to thank—people with whom, as it turned out, I had more in common than I had imagined. Every one of us entered our journey together with trepidation, not at all sure it would be a joyful part of our service to the church. But it turned out to be the most powerful experience of the Holy Spirit I had ever had, as a genuine sense of community formed among this very diverse group. An important part of our work was learning how to lower the decibel level—to speak our truths with love and respect, but also to listen to each other, to engage in genuine conversation, to really try to hear and understand another point of view.

The Bible had much to teach us about that and was indispensable to our engagement. Indeed, daily Bible study together whenever we met played no small role in the genuine sense of community that emerged among us and in our recognition of each other as fellow disciples of Jesus Christ. It was also an essential resource for our discernment on matters uniting and dividing our denomination. Every one of us experienced anew its power to shape and transform us as a community of faith. This book has emerged out of that experience and seeks to facilitate it for others.

The studies in the chapters that follow feature several of the biblical texts that we engaged as a group, but this book is not the work of the PC(USA)'s Theological Task Force on Peace, Unity, and Purity of the Church, and members of it should not be held responsible for the views articulated here, which are my own. (The collaborative document representing our consensus at the end of our journey is titled *A Season of Discernment: The Final Report of the Theological Task Force on Peace, Unity, and Purity of the Church to the 217th General Assembly (2006)* and can be found at http://www.pcusa.org/peaceunitypurity.) However, I am indebted to my task force colleagues for much that I learned about these texts in conversation with them. I am also indebted to many other Presbyterians throughout the denomination and in classrooms at Union-PSCE with whom I have engaged in reflection around these texts in recent years.

Seven Bible studies follow. Chapter 1 considers the practice of "arguing about Scripture" in connection with the Johannine epistles (1, 2, 3 John), which reflect the traumatic aftermath of a ferocious family quarrel about interpretation of Scripture. Both dangers and insights attested in these letters can inform our own practice of arguing about Scripture in our time and place. Chapter 2 examines the story of Jesus' and Peter's walking on the water (Matt. 14:22–33), which conveys significant affirmations about the identity of Jesus to and for the church, especially as it faces storms and attendant fears that conflict will undo us. Chapter 3 examines the apostle Paul's closing exhortation to the church at Rome (Rom. 14:1–15:13), where argumentative discourse is threatening the unity and stability of the church. Paul presents a fascinating discussion about living with disagreements, insisting that some things that appear to divide Christians deeply in terms of their practice are, in fact, "things indifferent" that are not essential for faith or salvation. Such differences do not need to be resolved. However, in some cases "essentials" are perceived to be at stake and differences must be adjudicated. And what are we to do when believers disagree about the Spirit's leading—when we find ourselves in conflict over our discernment of the will and work of God? Both the Old Testament and New Testament wrestle with the question of discernment, or "testing of spirits," and chapters 4 and 5 consider classic accounts of this wrestling, one from each testament (Jer. 28 and 1 Cor. 12–14). As ordination standards are the focus of conflict in many mainline denominations, chapter 6 considers a snapshot from the Pastoral Epistles (1 Tim. 3 and 5) of the early church's wrestling with qualifications and standards for church leadership. Chapter 7 considers, in closing, three central emphases of Jesus' farewell conversations in the Gospel of John (John 13–17) that bear on the experience of church conflict and communal discernment in the midst of it.

This book was designed for use by clergy, laypersons, and groups interested in substantive Bible study. I present technical matters in an accessible fashion and include study questions with each chapter to facilitate group discussion or individual reflection. Quotations of Scripture, unless otherwise noted, are from the NRSV. I hope that Christians wrestling with conflict of any kind may find in this volume a springboard for their own study and reflection—and that the Bible, by the power of the Holy Spirit at work within us, will continue to enable all of us engaged in ecclesial family feuds to live more faithfully with our disagreements and more fully into the peace, unity, and purity that is God's gift to us in Jesus Christ.

1

Arguing about Scripture: Johannine Epistles and Dirty Laundry

1 John 2:18–25; 1 John 4; 2 John

Have you ever found yourself arguing about Scripture? I invite you to think with me about this practice—one with considerable bearing on the peace, unity, and purity of the church. The Bible is one of the most important things that Christians have in common. We are held together in part by our conviction that this body of literature makes known God's identity and God's way with the world—that it brings us to salvation in Jesus Christ and guides us in our practice of the Christian life—that it is in fact "holy." As one of the position statements of my denomination affirms, "We call the books of the Bible 'Holy Scripture' because of the continuous experience of the church that God by the Holy Spirit confronts us and communicates with us through them."[1] Only rarely have I met a Christian who did not share these convictions.

But the Bible has also been a flash point for conflict in the church. Differing interpretations of it, over matters about which we care deeply, can become a source of disunity and enormous pain. So the Bible is something we have in common that creates us and sustains us as a community of faith, but it is also one of the things about which we argue fiercely.

I think it is important to note that we argue about the Bible precisely because it is important to us—because we are passionate about it. One does not argue about things one does not care deeply about. Indeed, there is actually something healthy about arguing about Scripture. It is a sign of the vitality and commitment and passion that are part of our life together. I contend that one of the challenges facing us is to frame this positively for the church.

To inform our reflection on this matter, I would like to direct your attention to the back of the New Testament. It would probably do us good to spend more time at the back of the book than we do. It seems to me that we usually hang out at the front, in the Gospels of Matthew, Mark, Luke, and John. This is familiar terrain: we know our way around their well-lighted streets and recognize familiar persons and places as they appear. We also venture past them now and then into Paul's letters, though here the going gets more difficult, for as the author of 2 Peter complained early on, "There are some things in them hard to understand" (2 Pet. 3:16). But we stay the course, tortuous though some of Paul's twists and turns may be, and make our way. Some of us foray beyond that as far as Hebrews, that most erudite of New Testament books, where we are likely to find ourselves bogged down completely in its complex and densely woven argument—mired in priestly imagery and sacrificial ritual. So we may not make it any further, to those little bitty letters at the back of the book such as 2 Peter and Jude, 1, 2, and 3 John. They don't get many visitors. They don't take up much space. But boy, they make a lot of noise. And if you venture down that much less traveled road, you will hear them yelling long before you get there. Fussing and fighting, a lot of name-calling going on: "You ain't nothing but a waterless cloud." "Yeah, well you ain't nothing but a dog that returns to its vomit." "Well, you are a blemish—a zit on the body of Christ!" "You're a liar, a deceiver— you're the antichrist!" As Fred Craddock has observed, "They really knew how to curse in those days."[2]

In fact, I find myself thinking of these little letters as the dirty laundry in the New Testament.[3] Maybe that is why the church has tucked them in at the back of the book. We all have dirty laundry, but we don't like to put it on display. We try not to air it in public because it doesn't smell very good. Some of it is frankly embarrassing.

But we all have it. Every family has dirty laundry. Who would deny that many mainline denominations have had a lot of dirty laundry piling up these last years? And much of it does not have about it what Paul would have described as "the aroma of Christ" (2 Cor. 2:15). We don't like to exhibit it to the general public's gaze. But it behooves us to reflect on it a bit, which is why I am pulling the Johannine Epistles out of the hamper for our consideration.[4] We believe that the books of the Bible are guides for us, and as Raymond Brown has observed, "Part of the guidance is to learn from the dangers attested in them as well as from their great insights."[5] Indeed, over the years I have come to appreciate Phyllis Trible's contention that the Bible is a mirror reflecting the whole panorama of life in both holiness and horror. The Bible, she says, has the authority of a mirror, for "you look in the mirror in the morning, and it shows you something you don't particularly like, so it gives you a choice to do something about it." It "sets before us blessing and curse, good and evil," and asks us to choose.[6] And both the blessings and curses—the dangers and insights that the Johannine letters hold before us—make for sobering reading for many Christians at this particular moment in our history.

ARGUING ABOUT SCRIPTURE: SNAPSHOT OF AN EARLY CHURCH

The little letters of 1, 2, and 3 John reflect the traumatic aftermath of a reality that many of us know all too well: a ferocious family quarrel. They emerge from the same community to which the Gospel of John was addressed, but reflect a different time frame in its history—ten years or so after the Gospel was written. Because we have both the Gospel and these later epistles, we can surmise a great deal about the internal history of this church.

And it is a tragic history. The Fourth Gospel has long been associated with the figure of an eagle, and so the picture we get of the church has been described like this: "In the Gospel the eagle soars above the earth, but with talons bared for the fray. In the Epistles we discover the eaglets tearing at each other for possession of the nest."[7] Both the Fourth Gospel and the Johannine Epistles, more clearly than other parts of the New Testament, bear signs of stress and conflict, but with different foci. In the Gospel we see a tightly knit early Christian community, wagons circled, focused on external conflict with the synagogue, from which it appears they have been ejected for their confession of faith.[8] But in the epistles the conflict has turned inward, and we find Christians turning their cannons on each other, and all the scathing vitriol once reserved for members of the synagogue is now directed at fellow Christians. Indeed, the community before us in these letters has been racked by schism. Our clearest glimpse of this is found in 1 John 2, where the author resorts to apocalyptic rhetoric to describe what he perceives as dire, cataclysmic circumstances: "Children, it is the last hour! As you have heard that antichrist is coming, so now many antichrists have come. From this we know that it is the last hour. They went out from us, but they did not belong to us; for if they had belonged to us, they would have remained with us. But by going out they made it plain that none of them belongs to us" (1 John 2:18–19). Conflict has given way to schism. A large faction of the community has withdrawn from fellowship, and in the painful aftermath of their departure, the author of 1 John seeks to bolster the confidence of the remnant that remains—whose faith has been shaken. Perhaps it should not surprise us that there is no sign of the community's earlier external conflict with the synagogue in the letters, for no conflict is as fierce and all-consuming as the family quarrel. We reserve a special rage for members of the family who cross us, betray us, offend us, disappoint us, or desert us, do we not? So it is not a pretty sight, this picture of eaglets tearing at each other for possession of the nest.

But there are both insights and dangers to consider as we eavesdrop on their squawking. This early Christian dirty laundry can surely illumine our own. And one of the insights that emerges from these little Johannine letters is that there are some things worth arguing about. I find it of interest that the two things over which they were arguing most vehemently are also on the laundry list of matters that my own denomination and many others have been disputing these last years: Christology and ethics. Indeed, as Clifton Black maintains in his fine commentary on 1 John, these letters compel us to consider that "some beliefs we may hold about Jesus are intolerably divergent from God's norm," and "that some activities in which we may engage are inescapably at odds with the One" in whom God is revealed.[9] What we confess about Jesus Christ and how we live in the household of God do matter—they matter profoundly. In fact, I suspect that all Christians who find themselves invested in current denominational conflicts are invested precisely because they believe that the integrity of the gospel is at stake.

I also find it of interest that the Johannine Christians appear to be arguing over a common tradition. At one time scholars believed that heretics, interlopers, outsiders, false teachers had infiltrated this community, leading some of its members astray. They have gone to great lengths to identify those intruders, usually as Docetists or gnostics of some stripe. However, it now appears much more likely that there are no outsiders or interlopers to blame, for none are ever mentioned in the letters— that rather, what the Johannine Christians are arguing about is how to interpret the Fourth Gospel itself, which they hold in common and all treasure. Indeed, Raymond Brown, a preeminent scholar on this literature, argued this rather persuasively (to my mind at least), pointing out that the Gospel of John "was relatively 'neutral' on some of the points that [came] into dispute, i.e., it did not contain direct answers, for these were new questions. In the tradition there were texts on both sides of the issue; so each of the disputing parties was making the claim that its interpretation of the Gospel was correct."[10]

It is not hard to imagine why traditions associated with the Fourth Gospel might have lent themselves to controversy over matters of Christology and ethics. In regard to the first, for example, there is no denying that the Fourth Gospel presents a very high Christology, that is, a portrait of Jesus that highlights his divinity and exalted status—"The Word became flesh and lived among us" (John 1:14)—but many who engage this Gospel regularly inquire as to whether Jesus' feet are really touching the ground, sensing that it does not do full justice to his humanity. And there is probably a good reason that Jesus' divinity outshines his humanity in John: it was likely the focus of the community's intense conflict with the synagogue. Affirmation of Jesus' humanity would not have placed the community's members in conflict with their compatriots, but confession of his divinity surely would have and may account for the fact that the Gospel focuses so heavily on this aspect of Jesus' identity. In short, this is what the first Johannine Christians, the charter members, were arguing about. They were so convinced that Jesus was the very revelation of God that they put themselves on the line for this confession, and having paid a price for it, they attached special importance to it. Jesus' divinity was thus the primary focus of their theological energies and reflection.

One can imagine that at a later date, at some remove from these events and as Gentile membership increased, the Fourth Gospel's bold affirmations took on new connotations, and some might have taken their christological reflection a bit too far— might have crossed a line. This, in fact, is the allegation articulated by the author of the Johannine Epistles as he speaks of a grievous error involving some kind of underestimation of Jesus' incarnation. We see this articulated clearly in 1 John 4:2–3: "Every spirit that confesses that Jesus Christ has come in the flesh is from God, and every spirit that does not confess Jesus is not from God." And also in 2 John 7 and 9: "Many deceivers have gone out into the world, those who do not confess that Jesus Christ has come in the flesh; any such person is the deceiver and the antichrist! . . . Everyone who does not abide in the teaching of Christ, but goes beyond it, does not have God." The author's opponents, in his view, have gone too far; they are progressives who have "gone beyond" the community's founding traditions. It cannot be said that progressivism in and of itself is anathema in the Johannine tradition, although Christians have often appealed to this verse to make the case that new thoughts are always bad thoughts.[11] But the Fourth Gospel itself offers a rather bold and innovative reinterpretation of the Jesus' traditions authorized by the work of the Paraclete (or Spirit), and as David Rensberger points out, the author of the epistles seeks "to guard the distinctiveness, the newness of Christian belief against retreat into a more commonplace understanding that saw flesh as unable to bring about divine salvation."[12] That, in fact, is the crux of the matter, for a close reading of the letters suggests that the author's opponents did not deny Jesus' humanity per se; as interpreters of the Fourth Gospel's traditions, they affirmed incarnation. But they erred in maintaining that Jesus' humanity, while real, had no salvific import.[13] This was the line they crossed—where they went too far. What was important, in their view, was Jesus' divinity and the revelation he brought, to which the author of the epistles makes a counterargument: that the way in which Jesus lived and the way in which Jesus died were also intrinsic components of redemption, and that failure to appreciate the full significance of Jesus' humanity has dire consequences for Christian faith.

One can also imagine how a reading of the Fourth Gospel could lead to differences of interpretation in the realm of ethics, for it is notably lacking in specific ethical instruction when compared with the Synoptic Gospels (Matthew, Mark, and Luke). About as close as we get to an ethical admonition in John is the command to "love one another," which appears rather late in the game.[14] Moreover, the Fourth Gospel's distinctive understanding of "sin" as "unbelief" might well have led believers to claims of sinlessness.[15] This may be why 1 John insists so emphatically that "if we say that we have no sin, we deceive ourselves, and the truth is not in us" (1 John 1:8). One can also imagine that underestimation of the significance of Jesus' humanity, the manner in which he lived and died, would have as a corollary underestimation of the significance of one's own discipleship—one's own embodied life of faith. So in

short, it is entirely plausible that the controversy reflected in
the Johannine Epistles was occasioned by differing interpretations of traditions associated with the Fourth Gospel. The
Johannine Christians were arguing about Scripture, for then as
now, Scripture is not self-interpreting. It is a living word
through which God continues to meet us and speak to us in
our own particular historical moment, and thus it demands to
be newly interpreted for new historical situations. Moreover,
interpretation is not simply reiteration of the text, but the hard
work of bringing it into our own time and place. Again, Raymond Brown has made a rather compelling case that the
Gospel of John was relatively neutral on points that came into
dispute at a later stage in Johannine history. It did not contain
direct answers for new questions. Texts on both sides of the
issue could be adduced; thus each of the disputing parties was
claiming that its interpretation of the Gospel was correct.[16]

ARGUING ABOUT SCRIPTURE
IN OUR OWN TIME AND PLACE

It is not easy when believers with good theological minds and
honest concern for the church find themselves in significant disagreement, having reached different conclusions from their
reading of the same Scriptures. I'm sure that folk on all sides of
the debates, then as now, feel that there is no ambiguity at all—
that their own view of the matter is quite self-evidently "the
truth"! We may even be tempted, as the author of 1 John clearly
was in chapter 4 verse 6 (not one of his better moments) to say,
"Whoever knows God listens to us, and whoever is not from
God does not listen to us. From this we know the spirit of truth
and the spirit of error." But if we take the time to listen to one
another, we may find ourselves surprised to learn that there is
actually a biblical and theological logic that led our "opponents"
to their conclusions—a biblical and theological integrity. They
did not reach them apart from a reading of Scripture and tradition. Indeed, it turns out that in my own denomination at least,

and perhaps in yours as well, we have been bearing false witness about fellow Christians with whom we disagree by continued propagation of inaccurate caricatures or stereotypes about how they read the Bible. For example, those of us who are "liberals" often allege that our conservative Christian kin are just proof-texting, reading very selectively (truth be known, we think they're downright fundamentalist, curiously lacking in any capacity for historical-critical reflection). And those of us who are "conservatives" all too frequently argue that "liberals" don't even care about the Bible—they consider it irrelevant.

But often these suspicions are not true and constitute false witness; at least, none of these creatures turned out to be present on the task force, which represented the broad spectrum of opinion in my own denomination, the Presbyterian Church (U.S.A.), nor have I encountered them in my travels around it. In the case of the task force, twenty Presbyterians who were as different from one another as we could possibly be, who never would have dreamed of hanging out together for five years, found we had to admit that every one of us honored Scripture and was striving as best he or she could to be faithful to it. And one of our other biggest surprises was that we did not live on different exegetical planets after all! We found unexpected agreement on basic principles of biblical interpretation—guidelines, methods, resources. We found that often we even agree on what Scripture says and on many points of interpretive detail, though some of our most serious disagreements focus on what constitutes faithful pastoral application of biblical teaching or on which passages of Scripture are relevant to a particular question.[17] For example, if the Bible doesn't have a whole lot to say about a matter with which we may be wrestling, all of us seem to recognize the need to engage a classic Reformed principle of biblical interpretation—that of interpreting Scripture by Scripture. We share that principle of interpretation. We all exercise it but can find ourselves disagreeing on *which* Scriptures are most relevant to questions at hand. We found, moreover, that this book really does have the power to shape and transform us as a community of faith, and that if you stop shaking it at each

other, open it, and actually read it in the company of believers
with whom you disagree—if you take the time to really listen to
one another—you may find yourselves surprised to learn that
there is a biblical and theological logic that led your "opponents" to their conclusions. You may not agree with their conclusions and consider them misguided, but you may have to
admit that their position is every bit as grounded in a reading of
the Scriptures and the Christian tradition as your own.

It is a genuine dilemma, and the one in which many of us
find ourselves today. In light of this, I was very interested to hear
Amy-Jill Levine make the following observation in her magnif-
icent book *The Misunderstood Jew*: "The general sense in the
Jewish tradition is that one argues with the text and with fellow
Jews about the text, and that in some cases multiple meanings
are possible. Jews are more inclined to say, 'I'm right, and you
may be right too.' Christians, more familiar with the word from
the pulpit, the hierarchy, or the individual (not just Jesus, but
Paul, Augustine, Aquinas, Luther, Calvin, Wesley, etc.), may be
more prone to seek a single response."[18] I think she is probably
right about that, and that we have much to learn from Jewish
friends about how to live more fully into the communal tension
of multiple interpretations, though it is surely also the case that
sometimes we do have to draw a line in the sand. In some cases
we can't all be right; some of us have to be wrong when the
integrity of the faith is at stake! That would appear to be the perception of the circumstance that many Christians believe we
face today, and it is why the author of 1 John urges us in every
age to "test the spirits": "Beloved," he writes, "do not believe
every spirit, but test the spirits to see whether they are from
God" (1 John 4:1). What this suggests is that the church ought
to be a place where we find "hard questioning" and "reasoned
deliberation about crucial matters of Christian faith and practice"—"an ongoing, evaluative enterprise."[19] It is one of the
most important reasons that believers need to stay together in
one body—to prevent schism and strengthen the ties that bind
us—not because the truth doesn't matter, but because it does,
and because "we need each other's different readings of Scrip-

ture. They broaden our vision; they help us to correct dis-
tortions in the lenses that we bring to the text."[20] Indeed, it is
important to understand that when we read in the Gospel of
John of the gift of the Holy Spirit, it is a gift to the whole community. John thinks of the Spirit present and speaking within
the community of the faithful—teaching us, reminding us of
what Jesus taught, and providing continuing guidance, even
about matters concerning which Jesus left no instructions.[21] "I
still have many things to say to you," Jesus said, "but you cannot bear them now" (John 16:12). And when he promises that
"the Holy Spirit, whom the Father will send in my name, will
teach you everything, and remind you of all that I have said to
you" (John 14:26), that "he will guide you into all the truth"
and "declare to you the things that are to come" (John 16:13),
all those "you's" are really "y'all's"—they are plural. This means
that we need each other to discern what God is calling us to be
and do. The "testing of spirits" that 1 John urges upon us is
communal discernment, and it is not easy. It evokes conflict,
but that conflict may well turn out to be the place of God's
guidance and activity among us. The Second Helvetic Confession, honored by Reformed Protestant communions, acknowledges as much when it says that God can use conflict "to the
glory of his name, to illustrate the truth, and in order that those
who are in the right might be manifest."[22] The eminent theologian Karl Barth makes the very same point when he argues that
we should not spare ourselves "relative conflict." John Burgess's
exposition of this important point is worth noting. Barth, he
says, reminds us that God's Word "rules over us all" and is "the
source of our unity," and that "an individual can never insist
that his or her hearing of Scripture is absolutely right. Barth
argues, nonetheless, that each of us must represent the Word
that we hear for ourselves, as best we can," noting that "we may
well come into conflict with each other, as we speak the different words that God has given us." We should not spare ourselves this "relative conflict," he says, because "only as we
grapple with each other's readings of Scripture will we discern
what form Christ is taking among us here and now."[23]

This requires, of course, the capacity to bear with each other's differences—what Bonhoeffer spoke of as "the ministry of bearing"[24]—and what the author of 1 John speaks of so repeatedly and so eloquently as love of one another. First John is the New Testament's most eloquent witness to love. Chapter 4 has been described as the most profound analysis of Christian love in the New Testament, surpassing even 1 Corinthians 13. But here we bump up against "the great anomaly" of 1, 2, and 3 John and the real dirty laundry, for the New Testament's most eloquent witness to love is so incredibly unloving in denouncing his opponents. "Liars!" he rants. "Deceivers! False prophets!" he rails. "Don't even greet them. Do not welcome them or receive them into your home. They are antichrists!"

The word "antichrist" appears only here in the New Testament, in these letters of John. This word, part of their legacy to us, is a word that grabs attention. Many years ago when I was a seminarian in Richmond, Virginia, there was a billboard south of town that intrigued me. You couldn't miss it when you were driving up I-95 into the city. It read: "The Anti-Christ: Who is it? Call 1-800-REALHOT." After years of driving by this billboard I finally couldn't stand it anymore—I had to call. So I dialed 1-800-REALHOT—and they wouldn't tell me! They did, however, want to sell me a book for $19.95 that would answer all my questions. I didn't want to know that badly. Whatever that book would have told me, the word "antichrist," in common parlance, has come to represent all that is demonic; it is the ultimate figure of evil and deception. There was a fairly common expectation among early Christians that some personification of evil, some final manifestation of opposition to God, would characterize the last days. The appearance of this apocalyptic image in the Johannine Epistles is thus striking in three respects. For one thing, the letters speak of antichrists in the *plural*. Secondly, these antichrists have already come. But the third and most striking thing about the deployment of this term is its use to describe and denounce ordinary human beings who are fellow Christians! It's the dirty laundry, the dangerous legacy of these letters—our tendency to demonize our opponents, brothers and sisters in Jesus Christ, to view them not merely as erring or misguided but in caricature fashion as demonic, as agents of evil and deception. Sharp polemic was common enough in the rhetoric of the first-century world, but throughout history church fathers, medieval theologians, Protestant reformers, Westminster divines, and others in their wake have found within this Johannine oratorical arsenal a sorry means by which to denounce other Christians. Sadly, to declare that believers we disagree with are simply not true Christians and never were to this day remains a common way of dealing with fundamental theological differences.[25] The problem with this, as David Rensberger has observed, is that once you've claimed your opponent is the devil, "it is no longer possible to consider what he or she says thoughtfully; there is no chance that any portion of their reasoning could be correct or worthwhile." It is no longer possible "that they could have any good intention of faithfulness to Christ."[26]

Has anyone called you demonic lately? Or have you heard yourself suggesting that a fellow member of your fellowship is simply not a true Christian and never was? At a recent presbytery meeting I attended, in the midst of heated, polarized debate over a contested motion, a member of the clergy came forward to share news of her recent trip to the Holy Land, the view from Mt. Carmel, and her conclusion from this experience: that fully half of the presbytery, those who disagreed with her, were prophets of Baal! Given that Elijah exterminated 450 of those prophets, I think people took it personally, and responses from the other side of the aisle were no more charitable. It was one of those experiences that confirmed for me the truth of that aphorism that goes, "Ministers are like manure. Spread them all around and they do a lot of good. But put them all in one place and sometimes they smell bad." I've always appreciated that insight, for occasionally it sheds a lot of light on presbytery meetings (and no doubt synod, district, and diocesan meetings as well).

THE PROBLEM WITH DIRTY LAUNDRY

Can you smell it? It's our dirty laundry and part of the Johannine Epistles' dangerous legacy to us, whenever they supply fuel for Christians who feel justified in hating other Christians for the love of God.[27] There are some things worth arguing about, and the "testing of the spirits" that the church must engage in in every age may entail the "relative conflict" of which Barth spoke. The problem is the manner in which we engage them, the manner in which we pursue the rigorous discernment required. That is the dirty laundry, and it is a serious problem. For one thing, it is dangerous for our own spiritual health, for as the author of 1 John himself insists: "Beloved, let us love one another, because love is from God; everyone who loves is born of God and knows God. Whoever does not love does not know God, for God is love" (1 John 4:7–8). In its finer moments, writes Rensberger, 1 John articulates with unsurpassed clarity that "God is revealed to us as love in Jesus the Christ" and that "we cannot accept or understand this revelation without taking upon ourselves the life of love for one another."[28] What this means is that true fellowship with the invisible God is visible, is manifest in a quality of life and character that can only come from God. So we cannot know God or claim fellowship with God while wearing dirty laundry. Indeed, along with adequate christological confession, the practice of love for fellow Christians within the church is held up as the key criterion for the testing of spirits, for failure to love invalidates any claim to know God.

But an even more serious problem is this: we don't look good in our dirty laundry. It mars our appearance and thus distorts our public witness in the world, for mutual love is the heart of the Johannine vision of the church—the identifying characteristic of the community that continues to exist in the world in Jesus' name. It is why Jesus in the Gospel of John commands that we love one another and prays that we might be one: so that the world will know that we are his disciples (John 17:20–26). He does not pray that we might all be the *same*, but that we might all be *one*, despite the differences that divide us, because the quality of our life together—our ability to make visible the unique relationship that exists by God's grace among us—is our most convincing witness to the truth and power of the gospel we proclaim.

Some lament the intracommunal limitation of this love commandment, for the Johannine tradition speaks not of love of neighbor or enemy but rather of "in-house" love, of Christians loving one another. But we ought not to dismiss the ethical seriousness of this commandment, for loving other Christians in this time and place may, in fact, be the most difficult thing that Jesus could have asked us to do. As the epistles remind us, love is hard as nails.[29] But it is what God through Jesus Christ has given us to know about God and to communicate to others, and there is a very real sense in which the love of God incarnate in Christ continues to be incarnate in the world in the life of the believing community—a community which stands as a sign of the light that shines in the darkness and has not been extinguished. Love of one another is therefore essential to the church's mission of making the presence and love of God real and known to the world. Lord knows that a violent and suffering world needs the healing power of the gospel—a gospel that makes a difference in how you deal with those with whom you disagree. The world needs our witness that if you've got it, you don't need to kill each other over differences.[30] But how is the world to glimpse that light if it does not see love for one another within our churches? It is, frankly, an embarrassing aspect of a good bit of Christian witness in the world at present, and the real problem with dirty laundry.

Having said this, we have to acknowledge the honest struggle on the part of many who are wrestling with the question of whether or not they can remain within their denominations. Those of us who are Protestants, at least, can hardly claim that schism is never called for. Surely forbearance and tolerance must finally have their limits when we perceive that the integrity of the faith is at stake. But prophetic wisdom is needed to determine when that time has come. For the Johannine community it clearly had, and in 2 and 3 John we see the church wrestling mightily with the question of defining the boundaries of its fellowship. The controversy that racked the Johannine community threatened to spread to satellite congregations as emissaries from both sides of the conflict sought a hearing, and it is to these satellite congregations, at some distance from the central community, that 2 and 3 John are addressed. These congregations faced a dilemma: how to deal with traveling missionaries who came their way. In 2 John 7–10, the elder issues a severe word of warning, recommending a policy of exclusion and negative hospitality: "Many deceivers have gone out into the world, those who do not confess that Jesus Christ has come in the flesh; any such person is the deceiver and the antichrist! Be on your guard. . . . Do not receive into the house or welcome anyone who comes to you and does not bring this teaching; for to welcome is to participate in the evil deeds of such a person." These words are among the least attractive in the Johannine corpus, and questions have been raised as to whether the elder violates the love command he advocates so urgently elsewhere. Moreover, his recommendation stands in marked contrast to the many other New Testament texts that commend hospitality as a key Christian virtue. But more than a snub, more than refusal of amenities, is in view, for hospitality was a mission strategy in the early church.[31] To receive traveling missionaries was to give them a foothold and a hearing in the house church, to provide a base of operation for further mission, and the author of 2 John clearly believes that a boycott is called for to protect the church—that love for fellow believers demands it (though he is mightily incensed in 3 John when the same policy is exercised against his own emissaries). But has your denomination or congregation reached this point? I can only speak with reference to my own, and I believe that we have not—that our current conflict is not yet a church-dividing one. For one thing, it appears that the integrity of our christological confession is intact and that the disagreements among us are disagreements among Christians. Fellow believers may be misguided or just plain wrong about some very important matters, but they are not infidels, and hospitality is surely required for the testing of spirits—for the genuine conversation and reasoned deliberation about these matters that must precede schism and exclusion.

Of course, some would say that we have talked long enough and it is time to leave. But the task force on which I served begged to differ. I think my colleague Victoria Curtiss said it best:

> We have debated for many years on some issues, but we have not engaged in substantive Bible study, theological reflection, and prayer with those with whom we differ. We have voted yes or no on some issues repeatedly, but we have not explored the full range of values, beliefs, concerns, hopes, and fears present within the church around those issues. We have sharpened our differences, but we have not articulated the theological convictions that bind us together. We have sought to gain or retain the majority vote for "our side," but we have not sought a common direction that moves us all forward. We have talked about gay and lesbian persons, but we have not knowingly included them in the conversation. We have taken formal disciplinary action against one another, but we have not first sought mediation and reconciliation. We have focused on the question, "Which side is right?" but we have not lived into the questions: "How is Christ at work through the multiplicity of voices?" and "How can we live together faithfully in the midst of our differences?"[32]

Could these observations describe your own experience of church conflict? Until we have had these conversations, we have not fully embraced the season of discernment and testing of spirits that the Johannine Epistles urge upon us.

Recently, Martin Marty of the University of Chicago, an astute observer of the American religious scene, was asked this question: "So how should our denominations deal with their conflicts over sexuality?" I was interested in his reply. He said, "Well, first, we need to stop voting on all of these issues, and rid ourselves of the fiction that majority rule in a 55–45 split reflects the will of God. And then we need to start practicing a new kind of polity, one rooted in conversation and hospitality."[33] And if

he's right about that, and I believe he is, we have got to do something about our dirty laundry problem.

TACKLING DIRTY LAUNDRY

So what should we do with it? The self-proclaimed "Queen of
Clean," Linda Cobb, maintains that dirty laundry is very
revealing and has identified four laundry personality types,
who tackle it with different mottoes. She says the first and most
common motto is "So much laundry, so little time." These folk
have perfected the art of multitasking. Appearance may be
important to them, but doing laundry is just a means to an
end. The second group lives by the motto: "Don't do laundry
today that you can put off until tomorrow." These are the laundry procrastinators who know every excuse in the book to put
off laundry, or get someone else to do it for them. The third
group lives by yet another motto: "If you want laundry done
right, you have to do it yourself." But the fourth school of
thought takes a different approach: "A little bit of dirt never
hurt anyone." They don't worry much about piles of dirty
laundry or their appearance, and they don't think twice about
wearing the same clothes days in a row.[34]

Of course, whatever our individual laundry personality
type, Christians share one further perspective on dirty laundry—a theological one. In our honest moments, we recognize
it as a reflection of our sin, a violation of our relationship with
God and one another. For as 1 John reminds us, "If we say that
we have no sin, we deceive ourselves, and the truth is not in us.
If we confess our sins, God who is faithful and just will forgive
us our sins and cleanse us from all unrighteousness" (1 John
1:8–9). So we all know what ultimately needs to happen with
dirty laundry: it needs to be washed!

I'm wondering then if Psalm 51, that most famous of penitential psalms, may be the best articulation of the good news
we need to hear, for as the psalmist knows, our sin, our dirty
laundry, is not the last word. To be sure, sin is a powerful, per-

sistent reality in our lives, but God's grace is a more powerful, enduring reality,[35] which is why the psalmist looks beyond self to God, laying hold of the marvelous possibilities of God's grace: "Have mercy on me, O God, according to your steadfast love; according to your abundant mercy blot out my transgressions. Wash me thoroughly from my iniquity, and cleanse me from my sin" (Ps. 51:1–2). What is most striking about this penitential psalm—which I hadn't noticed until James L. Mays helped me see it—is that although many of the prayers in the Psalter offer complaints against God or others, imploring God to "change my situation" or even to smite my enemy, in this one the psalmist prays, "Change me." I am the problem. Deliver me from the predicament of myself.[36] "Create in *me* a clean heart, O God, and put a new and right spirit within *me*. . . . Restore to *me* the joy of your salvation, and sustain in *me* a willing" or "generous spirit" (Ps. 51:10, 12).

This is a good place to start when tackling dirty laundry, as our task force discovered along our way. At the beginning I think most of us believed that the church's troubles were someone else's fault, but every one of us came to acknowledge our own contribution to current conflicts, to say we are sorry for the harm we have done to the church and to one another. It was a significant turning point in our life together, and our final report was a penitential document. Indeed, confessing our own sin for all the ways we have wounded the body of Christ is incumbent upon every one of us in the church. And once we have confessed our own sin, been blotted, washed, and cleansed by the grace of God, purged with hyssop until we are whiter than snow, what should we wear? In fact, isn't that really one of the most important questions in life? What in the world are we going to wear? Surely not dirty laundry! Perhaps our baptismal garments. We can put on Jesus Christ, for as the apostle Paul reminds us, "As many of you as were baptized into Christ have clothed yourselves with Christ" (Gal. 3:27). And one final bit of wardrobe advice from Colossians: "As God's chosen ones, holy and beloved, clothe yourselves with compassion, kindness, humility, meekness, and patience. Bear with

one another and, if anyone has a complaint against another,
forgive each other; just as the Lord has forgiven you. . . . Above
all, clothe yourselves with love, which binds everything
together in perfect harmony. And let the peace of Christ rule in
your hearts, to which indeed you were called in the one
body. . . . And whatever you do, in word or deed, do everything
in the name of the Lord Jesus, giving thanks to God the Father
through him" (Col. 3:12–17).

QUESTIONS FOR DISCUSSION OR REFLECTION

Why do you think Christians argue about Scripture?

Have you ever found yourself arguing about Scripture? If so,
what were you arguing about? And what did you learn
from that experience?

How would you describe your prior experience with the
Johannine Epistles (1, 2, and 3 John)? What role have
they played in your life of faith? In what contexts have
you encountered them?

The books of the Bible are guides for us. Do you agree with
Raymond Brown's observation that "part of that guidance is to learn from the dangers attested in them as well
as from their great insights"? Why or why not?

What strikes you most about the reading of the Johannine
Epistles presented in this chapter? What new insights did
it provide for you? What questions does it raise for you?

Think of church controversies in which you are, or have
been, engaged. Could it be said that there are biblical
texts on both sides of the issue and each of the disputing
parties is making the claim that its interpretation of
Scripture is correct? How so?

What caricatures or stereotypes have you used to speak of
your "opponents" in church controversies? What caricatures or stereotypes have they used to speak of you? Are
they accurate, or do they constitute false witness?

Share your reactions to Karl Barth's observation that we should not spare ourselves "relative conflict." Do you believe that conflict can turn out to be the place of God's guidance and activity among us?

The capacity to bear with each other's differences is crucial in the midst of communal discernment and the conflict it evokes. How might you exercise "the ministry of bearing" as you relate to your "opponents"? What, specifically, might this entail?

Has the "demonizing" of opponents characterized the church conflict in which you are, or have been, engaged? How so?

Do you share the conviction that dirty laundry is dangerous for our spiritual health and that it distorts the church's public witness in the world? Why or why not?

Do you believe that the gospel makes a difference in how you deal with those with whom you disagree? If so, how would you describe that difference?

Consider the observations by Victoria Curtiss on page 17. Do they describe the experience of church conflict in which you may be presently engaged? If so, how so?

We tend to think that the church's troubles are someone else's fault. How have *you* contributed to current conflicts, thereby wounding the body of Christ?

What has struck you most in your discussion or reflection on the Johannine Epistles and their bearing on the experience of communal discernment and conflict? How might insights you have gained inform your practice of arguing about Scripture?

2

Stepping Out of the Boat in the Midst of a Storm

Matthew 14:22–33

If it weren't for the Gospel of Matthew, we wouldn't know about Peter's walk on the wild side. I'm grateful that in Matthew the story of Jesus walking on the water is no longer a story of what Jesus alone can do. From Matthew's perspective, Jesus shares his power and authority with the church—so Peter walks on the water too! I'm also grateful for Matthew's clear-eyed realism about life in the church, for there may be no doubt that it is a picture of the church before us in this story as we consider this small boat filled with terrified disciples, battered by wind and waves on a storm-tossed sea. In fact, Matthew uses an odd word to describe what the waves are actually doing to the boat. Our translations convey that the boat was "battered" or "buffeted" by the waves. But a more literal translation would convey that the waves are actually "tormenting" the boat, "harassing" the boat, "torturing" the boat (*basanizomenon* in Greek). It is an odd description of what waves do to a boat, until you begin to see that this is much more than a story about a boat on the sea. It is a story about a tormented, conflicted church caught in the throes of a very difficult storm—fearful that the forces that blow through its life threaten to undo it and doubtful about the presence and power of the Lord.

So it seems that we are not the first disciples to find ourselves caught in a bad weather pattern. It is important to bear that in mind, for sometimes we are tempted to think that our storms, our conflicts, are more bitter, more intractable than any the church has faced before—but it's not true! Most of our denominational histories bear witness to the fact that we are fairly fractious people who have been fighting for a very long time. And neither were the earliest Christian churches models of irenic decorum, for Matthew was apparently well acquainted with conflict. A close reading of this Gospel leaves no doubt that it is addressed to a beleaguered church, weathering both external and internal threats to its life. Externally, for example, Matthew's church found itself in wrenching conflict with the synagogue—in the midst of a painful process of separation and self-differentiation. Internally, Matthew's church, much like our own, struggled mightily with church discipline and forgiveness, power plays, ethnic and ideological tensions, and what Matthew calls "love growing cold" (Matt. 24:12). So Matthew leaves us under no illusion that it is smooth sailing out there. Indeed, he holds before us a very realistic picture of the church in the midst of inclement weather, straining to be faithful in perilous times.

Matthew tells us that Jesus *made* those disciples get into that boat and sail out into that sea. They didn't get into the boat because they were necessarily a like-minded group of people who decided on their own accord to pursue a common endeavor together.[1] It was by *his command* that they found themselves together and on a mission. That is exactly how many people may find themselves engaged in the varied ministries of the church. They did not volunteer but rather were drafted. Sometimes the ministries in which we find ourselves engaged are not of our own choosing, and Jesus has to *make* us get into that boat. And so we may find ourselves sailing out amid the storms that buffet the church about. Sometimes we aren't altogether sure we really want to take the cruise—not at all sure it will be a joyful part of our service to the church. But there we are in the boat, perhaps in the company of believers we would rather not travel with; we may be very uneasy to be in close quarters with them with a long sail ahead. Fear may very well be a central reality we face as we undertake our journeys in ministry.

All of this was certainly the case for the twenty Presbyterians who set sail as the Theological Task Force on Peace, Unity, and Purity of the Church some years ago. Jesus had to *make* us get into that boat, through three formidable former moderators enlisted to commandeer us, for we were twenty Presbyterians as different as we could possibly be, who would never have dreamed of hanging out together for four years. Fear was a central reality we faced as we undertook our journey together, and we shared some of those fears as we came before this text that is filled with terrified disciples: Our fear of conflict. Fear of what this journey might cost us, personally and professionally. Fear of failure. And fear, above all, of the enormous risks we were being asked to take. In fact, we talked quite a bit about risk-taking that day, for it seemed to be what the story before us was about, and we realized that we too were being asked to take some very serious risks—to step out of the boat and to try something new we had never done before, trusting in the command of Jesus. One of the hardest things for me to get used to at first was the fact that the press corps came along for the ride, for as we tried to step out of the boat and ride the waves, attempting something we had never done before, they were in the back of the boat taking pictures! Indeed, throughout our journey, we were aware that the eyes of the whole church were upon us.

The fear and anxiety that can accompany our journeys in ministry may never completely go away—and to be honest, they never completely left us. But Jesus came among us, appearing in the midst of the storm, striding across its waters. And he said to us, "Take heart, I am; do not be afraid!"[2] "I am"—the same words that God spoke to Moses from the burning bush (Exod. 3:14). Only God can speak this way, which is exactly Matthew's point. Jesus came among us proclaiming his lordship over all creation and all that comes to pass. And it wasn't an apparition, a figment of our imaginations. Every one of us can now affirm with absolute certainty that *he was really there*—that he came to us whenever we opened the Scriptures to search together for what his spirit was saying to the church. He came to us whenever we worshiped and prayed together, whenever we shared his body and blood, the sign of our reconciliation with God and one another. He came to us reminding us again and again of how closely we are bound to him and one another through our baptisms in his name. And when he came, what we discovered about our fellow travelers, much to our surprise, was that every one of us *really did love him* and that every one of us was striving as best we could to be his faithful disciples. And so, like Peter, we decided to take some risks, to try to draw closer to him through new ways of discerning and learning together.

Did you ever wonder why Peter stepped out of the boat? I have a suspicion about that, for the church has been likened to Noah's ark in that if it weren't for the storm outside, we couldn't stand the smell inside. But I'm not so sure about that anymore, given the malodorous state of many of our own denominational boats at present. So I find myself thinking that maybe Peter needed some air! As noted in the last chapter, given the bad behaviors and polarizing rhetoric that have attended so much of current church conflict, the apostle Paul would be hard-pressed to describe many of our denominations at present as "the aroma of Christ" (2 Cor. 2:15). So I wonder if Peter had been to one too many tense, argumentative presbytery, synod, or diocesan meetings. You know the kind I am talking about: the kind where people line up at microphones on opposite sides of the room and begin shouting past one another, not even pretending to listen, caricaturing and even demonizing each other, saying things about brothers and sisters in Christ that should not be said. Maybe he needed some air. Asphyxiation was at least part of what compelled our task force to take a risk, for we knew something had to change, that our current manner of conducting our life together had become intolerable. It frankly stank.

But something else compelled Peter to step out of that boat and attempt walking on the water, something even more important: he wanted to be like Jesus. He wanted to emulate his

Lord—to imitate Jesus Christ. He really doesn't get enough credit for that, for sometimes it is said that he was being his impetuous, overconfident self—or even that he was testing Jesus. But as Barbara Brown Taylor has astutely observed, if he was testing Jesus, wouldn't a saner and safer test have been simply to ask Jesus something like, "If it's really you, tell us what we all had for supper tonight"?[3] Peter wasn't testing Jesus. There are, in fact, a lot of different ways to say "if" in Greek, but what Peter said bordered on "*since* it is you, command me to come to you on the waters."[4] He gave expression to his faith and to an entirely appropriate desire to emulate his Lord, not just in intention but in action. He wanted to imitate Jesus Christ. Moreover, he didn't vault impetuously over the gunwales. He waited for the command of Jesus, for enabling grace. And Jesus didn't reprimand him for his request. He didn't say, "*Now* you've really gone too far." He said to Peter, "Come." So Peter stepped out of the boat and took a few faltering steps upon the waves. And so it was for our task force as we risked finding ways to live more faithfully with our disagreements—new ways of learning and discerning together—for we wanted to be like Jesus too, to draw closer to him. And, like Peter, we didn't always walk on the water successfully. Our own steps were faltering, for sometimes the noise and power of the storm would distract us and scare us, and in those moments, whenever we took our eyes off Jesus, we too would begin to sink beneath the waves. But just when we were about to go under, we would inevitably find his saving hand upon us—and also face his reprimand, his challenge: "You of little faith, why did you doubt?" He never said, "You of little faith, *why* did you attempt to walk on the water?" Instead he said, "You of little faith, why did you doubt that you could?" Both his grace and his judgment accompanied us, as they did Peter, every step of the way.

People said it was a miracle that twenty Presbyterians as different as could be could learn how to love one another. And miracle of miracles, we produced a unanimous report—the only PC(USA) task force or special commission in living memory with controversial issues on its agenda to do so, to issue a statement not accompanied by a minority report! It's a miracle! It's walking on water!

People have also said, "Yeah, but this will never happen in my church, in my presbytery. You don't really think, do you, that the task force's experience can be replicated throughout the church? Impossible! There is no way we'll ever be able to walk on water too."

But of course there is, for we had to fly across the country to meet together, whereas all the diversity present on our task force is in your presbytery, synod, or diocese—maybe also in your congregation—right in your own backyard! More importantly, Jesus Christ, the Lord of all creation and of all that comes to pass, continues to share his power and authority with his church. And disciples still long to draw close to him and to emulate their Lord. But here's the thing: it requires a risk. You've got to step out of the boat and attempt something you may never have done before. I won't kid you about this. It is not easy—it is hard to do. It is a risk that takes time and energy and commitment—the disciplines of patience and forbearance. And Matthew won't kid you either. He would have us understand that the church will continue to face storms ahead, and in the midst of them we will continue to wrestle with our doubts and fears—with our "little faith"—for that is the way it is for disciples in this world. But a little faith is really all it takes, for Jesus promised that if you have faith even the size of a mustard seed, you can move a mountain!

Israel's National Parks Authority has authorized construction of a submerged bridge on the Sea of Galilee that will allow tourists to simulate Jesus' miraculous walk on water. The span will be built at Capernaum, the site where tradition says Jesus' walk on water took place. The 13-foot-wide, 28-foot-long floating bridge will be submerged two inches below the water's surface and will accommodate up to fifty people. To enhance the effect, it will not have handrails. Lifeguards and boats will be on hand in case a walker slips off.[5]

But you really don't need to travel to the Holy Land to simulate the experience. You can take that risk here and now, wherever believers gather in Jesus' name. Take heart, do not be afraid!

Step out of the boat and join us out on the water that we may draw closer to Jesus together. He's a lifesaver; he'll be on hand when we need him, with his word of judgment and his saving grace. And when he lifts us above the waves and puts us back in the boat where we belong, let's stay together in it and kneel before the Son of God, bound in worship, thanks, and praise.

GROUP STUDY SUGGESTIONS

Matthew 14:22–33 is a dramatic text that deserves a dramatic reading. Assign roles to a narrator, to Jesus, and to Peter, and have the rest of the group read collectively the lines of the other disciples (including nonverbal responses and sound effects).

Following the reading, ask participants to share their first impressions: What struck you most as you heard the story, and what questions does it raise for you? Remind participants that the text is two thousand years old, from another time and place. Ask: What is familiar about the experience reflected in the story? What is strange? What connections and gaps between the text's world and ours do you discern?

A good storyteller will draw attention to important matters by way of repetition. What are some of the repeated words or concepts in the story? Make a list.

One other preliminary exercise will enhance your engagement with this story. The evangelist Mark was the first to record it (Mark 6:45–52). As the evangelist Matthew retold it to his own community some years later, he reshaped, altered, and edited the story to address issues of concern in his community and to give expression to his own theological convictions. Divide your groups into pairs, and have them compare both accounts of the story (see parallel accounts below): What differences emerge from the comparison? What significant editorial changes do you observe in Matthew's rendition? After completing this exercise, have pairs compare notes with the whole group on the editorial fingerprints they discerned. This will help your group appreciate Matthew's distinctive contribution to this old, familiar story.

Mark 6:45–52

Immediately he made his disciples get into the boat and go on ahead to the other side, to Bethsaida, while he dismissed the crowd. After saying farewell to them, he went up on the mountain to pray.

When evening came, the boat was out on the sea, and he was alone on the land. When he saw that they were straining at the oars against an adverse wind, he came towards them early in the morning, walking on the sea. He intended to pass them by. But when they saw him walking on the sea, they thought it was a ghost and cried out; for they all saw him and were terrified. But immediately he spoke to them and said, "Take heart, it is I; do not be afraid." Then he got into the boat with them and the wind ceased. And they were utterly astounded, for they did not understand about the loaves, but their hearts were hardened.

Matthew 14:22–33

Immediately he made the disciples get into the boat and go on ahead to the other side, while he dismissed the crowds. And after he had dismissed the crowds, he went up the mountain by himself to pray. When evening came, he was there alone, but by this time the boat, battered by the waves, was far from the land, for the wind was against them. And early in the morning he came walking toward them on the sea. But when the disciples saw him walking on the sea, they were terrified, saying, "It is a ghost!" And they cried out in fear. But immediately Jesus spoke to them and said, "Take heart, it is I; do not be afraid."

Peter answered him, "Lord, if it is you, command me to come to you on the water." He said, "Come." So Peter got out of the boat, started walking on the water, and came toward Jesus. But when he noticed the strong wind, he became frightened, and beginning to sink, he cried out, "Lord, save me!" Jesus immediately reached out his hand and caught him, saying to him, "You of little faith, why did you doubt?" When they got into the boat, the wind ceased. And those in the boat worshiped him, saying "Truly you are the Son of God."

Proceed with any of the questions for discussion and reflection.

QUESTIONS FOR DISCUSSION AND REFLECTION

What new insights or questions emerged for you in the reading of the story presented in this chapter?

The church to which the Gospel of Matthew was addressed was struggling mightily with both external and internal conflicts. Externally, Matthew's largely Jewish-Christian congregation was engaged in vigorous conflict with the synagogue as it navigated a painful transitional process of separation and self-differentiation (Matt. 23). Internally, it wrestled with church discipline and forgiveness (Matt. 18), false teachers and prophets (Matt. 7:15–20; 24:11, 24), people with authority problems (Matt. 23:8–10), ethnic and ideological tensions (Matt. 15:21–28), and love growing cold (Matt. 24:12). How does this historical setting illumine your reading of the story? What storms and conflicts does your community of faith face at present, and what does the story contribute to your reflection upon them?

Why do you think Peter stepped out of the boat?

How do you imagine the tone of Jesus' voice in his response to Peter in verse 31: "You of little faith, why did you doubt?"

There is a great deal of Old Testament background music in this text. What Old Testament echoes do you hear, and what do they convey? What do they contribute to a reading of the story? (Study Bibles will be of assistance.)

There are important connections between this scene and two other scenes in Matthew's Gospel. Compare this story in 14:22–33 with the stories that appear in 8:23–27 and 28:16–20. What connections do you observe?

Where are you in this story? With whom do you most identify, and why?

What connections do you discern between this story and your life—and the life of your congregation or denomination?

What do you learn from this story about the nature of discipleship and the life of the church?

What do you learn from this story about Jesus? Share your reaction to Matthew's conviction that Jesus shares his power and authority with the church.

As you navigate storms in your own life or ecclesial setting, in what ways do you most yearn to imitate Jesus Christ? At what points are you hearing his word of judgment? In what ways are you experiencing his saving grace?

Where do you and/or your community of faith find yourself challenged to take risks—to get out of the boat and onto the water, taking steps toward greater faith and obedience?

Consider this quotation from New Testament storyteller Tom Boomershine, and share your responses to it:

This story addresses the primal fears that cripple us as human beings and as followers of Jesus. These are fears of the power of chaos in its many and varied forms, from the uncontrollable powers of nature to the irrational forces that suddenly arise from the depths of our personal and communal lives. Symbolized as storms, wind, and ghosts, these unknown forces of chaos blow through our lives. And the fear of these powers often leads us into weak resignation, cowardice, and withdrawal. This story is an experience of testing those powers, discerning who is truly in control, and taking the first steps toward true discipleship. It sets those fears in the context of Jesus' power, which he both exercises on our behalf and offers to those who believe in him.[6]

Boomershine asks groups exploring the story this question: "In what way are you now experiencing fears of the unknown or are doing something you have never done before and are afraid you will lose it?"[7]

What new insights have emerged from your engagement with the story of walking on water? What questions would you like to ask Jesus, Peter, or each other?

3

Living with Disagreements
Romans 14:1–15:13

The apostle Paul's closing exhortation to the church at Rome includes a fascinating discussion about living with disagreements, addressed to Christians whose argumentative discourse is threatening the unity and stability of the church. What are they arguing about? It seems that there are, within the house churches of Rome, different understandings of what proper response to the gospel of Jesus Christ looks like. The main point Paul tries to convey to these congregations, writes N. T. Wright, is that "there are some things that appear to divide Christians very deeply in terms of their practice but are, in fact (in the language of later theology), 'things indifferent' that should not be allowed to divide them."[1] Such matters are clearly very important to the disputing parties, but from Paul's perspective are not essential for faith or salvation. Indeed, says Paul Achtemeier, Paul maintains that "there is room within the Christian community for differing ways of responding to the gospel with respect to one's everyday life."[2] The problem he perceives is when one group tries to impose its understanding of Christian faith and lifestyle on others.

Paul is *not* suggesting that "anything goes." There are limits to Christian behavior, as we know from his discussion elsewhere. In

1 Corinthians, for example, he is fit to be tied about sexual immorality (a man living with his father's wife; 1 Cor. 5) and divisive worship practices (1 Cor. 11). But what Paul *is* saying in Romans 14–15 is that within the structures of grace (and limits of acceptable behavior) there is a measure of freedom.[3] Therefore, Christians must exercise forbearance as they live together with differences and disagreements over what proper response to the gospel looks like.

What occasioned Paul's extended discussion of this matter? The situation of the church at Rome has been a matter of debate. Some scholars think that the circumstances Paul addresses are hypothetical rather than real, that Romans 14:1–15:13 represents general reflection growing out of his pastoral experience in Galatia and Corinth—general pastoral advice about typical issues facing the life of early Christian communities. However, most scholars are now persuaded that this text is quite situation-specific. Paul has never visited Rome before, but he knows a number of Christians there (see Rom. 16) and has heard much about the Roman house churches that is of concern to him. Thus, he devotes a great deal of space at the end of the letter to discussion of a major social and theological problem threatening the stability and the unity of the church at Rome—one that he believes subverts the gospel. Indeed, he devotes more space to discussion of this ethical matter than to any other in the letter, so it is one of considerable significance to him.

Two antagonistic groups are identified by label in this text: the "weak" on the one hand, and the "strong" on the other. We can be fairly certain that the "weak" did not identify themselves as such! (Can you imagine: "We're the weak!" "Let's hear it for the weak!") This is probably the terminology of the "strong" and reflects their stereotypical grasp of the situation—a viewpoint, even caricature, that would hardly have been welcomed by the "weak."[4] Paul adopts this language of "weak" and "strong" and clearly identifies with the "strong" in 15:1. But to be fair, let us keep in mind that the "weak" might have described things differently. (It would be interesting to know what labels they were using to describe both themselves and members of the other camp.)

What do we know about the "weak" and the "strong"? They seem to have very different opinions about food and drink and the observance of special days. A major bone of contention appears in 14:2: "Some believe in eating anything, while the weak eat only vegetables." Another is mentioned in 14:5: "Some judge one day to be better than another, while others judge all days to be alike." Their disagreements center on dietary scruples (purity matters) and the observance of certain holy days (the Sabbath, perhaps, or other festival days), which suggests that traditional Jewish sensitivities are in view. Thus, one thing at stake in the dispute over food and special days is the continuing importance of these observances, given their traditional importance as integral parts of Jewish heritage.[5]

But a few caveats are needed. For one thing, the Mosaic Law does not prohibit the eating of meat or drinking of wine, though Jews in non-Jewish contexts often restricted their diets to avoid violating dietary scruples (as did Daniel and his friends when in Nebuchadnezzar's custody; Dan. 1). Also, most scholars would caution us against assuming that the "weak" were all Jewish Christians and the "strong" were all Gentile Christians. Paul, for example, was a Jewish Christian, but he counts himself among the "strong" who no longer observe dietary laws, and the same was probably true of Prisca, Aquila, and other Jewish Christians. And among the "weak" were no doubt Gentiles who practiced vegetarianism, perhaps to distance themselves from their former way of life and its idolatrous practices. We know from Paul's letter to the Galatians that dietary prescriptions and observance of particular days had appeal for some Gentile Christians. Thus, we should not think in terms of a clear-cut ethnic split. No doubt, both "strong" Jewish Christians and "strong" Gentile Christians were in one camp, and "weak" Jewish Christians and "weak" Gentile Christians in the other. Interestingly, Paul nowhere uses the word "Jew" or "Gentile" in 14:1–15:6 (shrewdly, no doubt, to avoid reinforcing ethnic divisions); it is only in the final paragraph

(15:7–13) that specific references appear, as Paul describes Christ's service to both Jews and Gentiles. Still, one cannot help but suspect a strong element of Jewish-Gentile tension behind the divisions—a tension that underlies much of this entire letter. Since dietary scruples and observance of holy days may strike us today as trivial matters, we may need to remind ourselves that they were crucial and highly sensitive ones in early Christian communities. For Jewish Christians, these practices had been part of their lifelong formation as God's covenant people and were key markers of distinctive identity; thus, deeply rooted cultural issues and identity questions were at stake.

Political realities may have exacerbated these divisions. The first Christians in Rome were Jews, but in the year 49 CE, the Emperor Claudius expelled the Jews from Rome (including Jewish Christians). When the edict of Claudius was lifted in the year 54 and Rome's Jewish population returned, Jewish Christians would have returned to a church that had become largely Gentile in the intervening years—a church with a very different composition and ethos. Returning Jewish Christians may have had difficulty adapting to the new situation and finding genuine acceptance[6]—perhaps difficulty finding a kosher butcher as well. Indeed, it is worth noting that "welcome one another" is the key admonition in Romans 14–15. The fact that such admonishment is needed suggests this is *not* happening, that they are meeting separately, not worshiping together, and nursing antagonism and suspicions about one another. While we are in the realm of historical speculation, scholars now generally agree that the return of Jewish Christians to Rome and tensions between predominantly Jewish house churches on the one hand and predominantly Gentile house churches on the other illumine the conflicts addressed in Romans 14–15. As N.T. Wright puts it, this historical scenario is one "into which Romans fits like a glove."[7] Recently the possibility that "weak" and "strong" may also have had social connotations has been discussed—that tensions related to social class and status may have accompanied the theological ones.

Perhaps the "strong" included more card-carrying Roman citizens who occupied a higher rung on the socioeconomic ladder.[8] (Classism has been known to infiltrate the life of the church and exacerbate conflict!)

In terms of its literary context, Romans 14:1–15:13 appears at the end of a long section of ethical exhortation (chaps. 12–15) in which Paul develops the ethical implications of the whole argument he has been making throughout the letter. This text is the climax of Paul's ethical exhortation, and in many respects it is also the conclusion to the whole letter. Both its position in the letter and the space devoted to it indicate that the matter at hand is one of real importance to the church at Rome—indeed, writes James Dunn, "one whose resolution was integral to Paul's own understanding of the gospel and its corporate outworking."[9] Among the words immediately preceding this text are these: "Owe no one anything, except to love one another" (13:8) and "Put on the Lord Jesus Christ, and make no provision for the flesh, to gratify its desires" (13:14). In chapter 14, Paul begins to talk very specifically about what "putting on the Lord Jesus Christ" and "love" mean in practice within the life of the Christian community.

I recommend that you stop at this point and read through this lengthy text, pausing to collect your impressions of it and, if you are engaged in group study, to share these impressions with others. What strikes you most as you hear this text? What questions does it raise for you? As there is a great deal of repeated language in the text, you may also want to take note of the concepts that are underlined by way of repetition. What words strike you as particularly important as you think about the language Paul is using? I offer observations below as food for continued thought.

ATTITUDINAL ADJUSTMENT

The text presents a variety of perspectives worth pondering in the midst of church conflict. One of the most important is the self-reflection to which it calls us with respect to the attitudes we display toward those with whom we disagree. Among the words that appear most repeatedly throughout the text are those that describe inhospitable attitudes toward brothers and sisters in Jesus Christ. Indeed, their differences in lifestyle are not Paul's concern, for he makes no effort to adjudicate the particular matters of dispute. While he has his own opinion about them (as a self-identified, card-carrying member of the "strong" faction), he does not weigh in on the debate and attempt to persuade the "weak" to his own point of view; he does not insist on a single mode of orthopraxis. He is far more concerned about the antagonistic, intolerant attitudes believers display toward the differences in their midst, and he calls for attitudinal adjustment.

The psychological insights Paul displays about these attitudes are remarkably contemporary. He speaks, in particular, of "judging" on the one hand and of "despising" on the other. "Those who eat" apparently need to be exhorted "not to *despise* those who abstain" (they quite literally "make absolutely nothing" of them or "treat them as nobodies," for the Greek verb *exoutheneō*, derived from *outhen* ["nothing"] and the prefix *ex*, carries a clear note of arrogance and contempt).[10] "Those who abstain" need to be exhorted to "not *pass judgment* on those who eat" (14:3, 10). These perennial attitudes of "judging" and "despising" plague church relations to this day. Indeed, James Dunn discerns in them a clash of two fundamentals: that of constitutive tradition and practice on the one hand, and that of liberty of faith in Christ on the other:

> The language is very striking and reveals a penetrating insight on Paul's part into the psychology of group conflict. As repeated experience within Christian history reminds us, those who stand on the fundamental of Christian liberty will be tempted to "despise," to hold in contempt the more traditional—to despise them for what "the strong" regard as the narrowness of their scruples. At the same time, those who stand on the fundamental of constitutive tradition will tend to "judge" or condemn the more liberal—or judge

them because they regard "the strong" as having abandoned or fatally compromised the *bene esse* if not the *esse* itself of Christian tradition and identity.[11]

Likewise, Luke Timothy Johnson notes the continuing relevance of Paul's observations: "The attitudes Paul identifies are amazingly contemporary—or perhaps are simply perennial for intentional communities. Who has not lived in a community in which 'conservatives' who swear by the law stand in judgment on the 'liberals,' and the liberals who glory in their freedom hold the conservatives in disdain?"[12]

In both cases, serious attitudinal adjustment is called for, for a whole host of reasons, not the least of which is the status of the fellow believer whom we judge or despise as one whom God in Christ has welcomed—indeed, one for whom Christ lived and died. Christ, as risen Lord, has claimed that fellow believer as his own; thus, who are we "to pass judgment on servants of another? It is before their own lord that they stand or fall" (14:4). Moreover, as Paul pointedly reminds his readers, "We will all stand before the judgment seat of God" (14:10). Do we dare, then, usurp the prerogatives of God and the lordship of Jesus Christ, rendering judgments that are not ours to make? Instead, we would do well to examine our own disposition and demeanor, for ultimately both will come under divine scrutiny—indeed, "each of us will be accountable to God" (14:12). Katherine Grieb states the implication pointedly, lest we miss it: "Paul argues that Christians are just as accountable to God for their *attitudes* towards their brothers and sisters with whom they disagree as they are accountable for the *decisions* they have made that divide them from one another."[13]

Paul focuses the minds of his readers especially on the lordship of the risen Christ, for to despise or judge fellow believers is to lose sight of who he is.[14] The Greek word *kyrios*, or "lord," appears ten times in the first eleven verses, underlining the lordship of Jesus Christ as the central consideration in any evaluation of the Christian life. Believers belong to him, orient every aspect of their existence to him, and derive validation from him: "For to this end Christ died and lived again, so that he might be Lord of both the dead and the living" (14:9).[15] And in this respect, different though the lifestyles of the "weak" and "strong" may be, neither is without integrity, for both seek to honor the Lord (14:5–6)—the "strong" by "eating" and the "weak" by "not eating." In both cases, their conduct is determined by faith and offered to God in thankfulness—Paul's "rule of thumb" for acceptable Christian conduct.[16] He thus calls both the "weak" and the "strong" to recognition of the integrity of the other's position and practice—indeed, to acknowledge each other as Christians and respect each other's convictions.

The "weak" and the "strong" may also have to admit that they have more in common than they might have imagined—a point usually overlooked in the midst of conflict, when "differences" seem paramount. But Paul's evenhanded discussion squarely locates both camps in the same boat: both give allegiance to Jesus as Lord, both seek to honor and give thanks to God, and both share in the life of the kingdom. Both also have duties toward each other, and both are in danger of allowing their convictions to disrupt Christian fellowship.

Moreover, the "weak" have no less a grasp than the "strong" of the basic content of the faith, namely, Jesus' resurrection and lordship.[17] In fact, Romans 14:1 does not necessarily refer to the "weak" as "weak in faith" (as translations often assume: "Welcome those who are weak in faith" [NRSV] or "Accept him whose faith is weak" [NIV]). As Katherine Grieb points out, the phrase "in faith" could just as easily characterize the welcome that is to be extended: "Accept" or "Welcome in faith (or faithfulness) those who are weak."[18] But whatever the case may be, says N. T. Wright, the "weakness" in view does not imply religious devotion that is "thin and watery" or "a shaky grasp of the basic points of Christian faith."[19] He explains: "[Paul's] point, rather, is that they have not worked out, or not as fully as he and some others have done, the consequences of believing in God as creator and Jesus as the crucified and risen Lord."[20] What they are doing is not *wrong*, but rather akin to driving 35 miles per hour in a 55 miles per hour zone.

So interestingly, Paul allows for the fact that "genuine Christians grow to maturity at different rates and that during this process one cannot and must not hurry or harry them to accept positions their conscience at the moment cannot allow."[21] One gets the sense, however, that the "weak" are in fact being harried, browbeaten—that considerable social pressure is being exerted upon them, for the opening admonition urges the "strong" to welcome them, "but not for the purpose of quarreling over opinions" (14:1). To coerce fellow believers into eating something they have genuine doubts about, in violation of conscience, is to do serious injury to them, for "whatever does not proceed from faith is sin" (14:23). Christians are thus under obligation to honor and protect the consciences of fellow believers.

THE MINISTRY OF BEARING

The Christians in Rome are given a clear picture of negative attitudes and behaviors that must cease (despising, judging, browbeating, quarreling over opinions). But Paul also turns to positive exhortations, describing constructive attitudes and actions that make "for peace and for mutual upbuilding" (14:19), and what he describes looks much like what Dietrich Bonhoeffer called "the ministry of bearing."[22] This is obscured somewhat by unfortunate translations of 15:1, which convey that "the strong" "ought to put up with the failings of the weak" (e.g., NRSV). This translation is infelicitous on two counts. For one thing, the Greek verb *bastazein* urges Christians not simply to put up with or to grudgingly tolerate each other, but rather (more actively and positively) to bear with or support each other. The NIV, for example, translates, "We who are strong ought *to bear with* the failings of the weak." However, Paul has not suggested that weakness is a failing, and this is the second point at which revision is needed. The Greek phrase in question is *ta asthenēmata tōn adynatōn*. The first word is related to the verb *astheneō*, which Paul has used to refer to the "weak" and conveys "weakness," "illness," or "limitation"[23]; the second word, *adynatos*, literally means "powerless." So Paul exhorts the "strong" to bear the weaknesses of the powerless, along the lines of Galatians 6:2: "Bear one another's burdens." As Leander Keck observes, "By speaking of 'weaknesses' Paul shifts the focus from persons to their incapacities, to their inhibitions, their inability to be fully convinced that all victuals are indeed 'clean' (14:20)."[24] The Revised English Bible conveys 15:1 in this manner: "Those of us who are strong must accept as our own burden the tender scruples of the weak."

Paul would appear to place the burden of responsibility on the "strong." For perhaps the first time in his career, he finds himself in the unusual position of defending Jewish sensibilities against Gentile ones and trying to curb the intolerance of those who share his own point of view.[25] Though he believes that all foods are in fact clean, he urges members of his own camp to forgo eating controversial foods in the presence of "weak" brothers or sisters lest their consciences be wounded: "If your brother or sister is being injured by what you eat, you are no longer walking in love. Do not let what you eat cause the ruin of one for whom Christ died" (14:15). They are to forbear (and forgo eating), explains Keck, "not because the vegetarians are 'sensitive' folk who are easily offended, but because their convictions too are rooted in faith."[26] Moreover, in so doing they *exercise* (rather than *sacrifice*) their freedom.[27] In short, it would appear that in Paul's view, "rights" take a backseat to "responsibilities." Commitment to the well-being of brothers and sisters in Christ (and thus responsibility for them) takes precedence over "rights" one might be tempted to exercise. It even takes precedence over "being right." Indeed, the standpoint from which Paul speaks is an astonishing one, succinctly put by Keck: "Being right is not the most important thing."[28] For when we insist on being right, we "live to ourselves" rather than to the Lord (14:7–8).

"Each of us must please our neighbor for the good purpose of building up the neighbor" (15:2). The Lord Jesus himself provides the norm for this ministry of forbearance that Christians are to exercise with each other, for with considerable understatement Paul reminds his readers, "Christ did not please himself" (15:3). Throughout his life and especially in his death, Christ modeled self-giving and self-limitation in commitment to the well-being of others. Paul's exhortation to the church at Rome resonates with one he penned earlier to the church at Philippi: "Let each of you look not to your own interests, but to the interests of others. Let the same mind be in you that was in Christ Jesus, who, though he was in the form of God, did not regard equality with God as something to be exploited, but emptied himself, taking the form of a slave, being born in human likeness. And being found in human form, he humbled himself and became obedient to the point of death—even death on a cross" (Phil. 2:4–8). In Romans, however, Paul appends to his exhortation a sobering text from Psalm 69:9 (LXX 68:10): "The insults of those who insult you have fallen on me" (15:3). He may very well be suggesting that the insults believers inflict on each other in the midst of church conflict fall upon Christ himself, adding to the reproach he bore on the cross for the sake of all.[29] Surely this should compel us to bridle our lips whenever contemptuous, judgmental sentiments might otherwise find expression. As we strive to exercise the admittedly challenging ministry of forbearance, we are ever in need of the instruction and encouragement of the Scriptures (15:4), as well as the divine assistance for which Paul prays: "May the God of steadfastness and encouragement grant you to live in harmony with one another, in accordance with Christ Jesus, so that together you may with one voice glorify the God and Father of our Lord Jesus Christ" (15:5–6).

REFRAMING CHURCH CONFLICT:
THE BIG PICTURE

Conflict has the tendency to constrict the horizons of our vision. When we are immersed in it, all else recedes from view. Indeed, it is hard to imagine any party to a fierce conflict conceding that the matter of dispute is an ultimately "indifferent" or "nonessential" one. We often find ourselves in conflict precisely because matters of essential importance appear to be at stake and we are heavily invested in the outcome. While from our contemporary vantage point the matters in dispute in first-century Rome (dietary restrictions and calendar observances) hardly seem essential to Christian faith, they were deemed crucial at the time, bearing on significant questions of identity and the shape of Christian freedom. Perhaps it is well to consider the possibility that future generations of Christians will look back on our own all-important and all-consuming squabbles with bemusement or perplexity. Time will tell.

But whatever the case may be, Paul provides an indispensable theological framework within which to locate church conflict in any age. Indeed, he lifts our eyes to the eschatological horizon, inviting us, says Richard Hays, to "look up and into the future that has broken in upon us"[30]—to take in the big picture and to reframe our squabbles in light of it. That big picture is the larger biblical narrative of God's cosmic project of reconciliation, embodied in the life of the covenant people Israel and realized in the death and resurrection of Jesus Christ. As risen Lord, Christ reigns within the church where he is confessed and where his resurrection power is at work, creating a "strange new community in which Jew and Gentile, slave and free, male and female stand together in harmonious praise of the one God of Israel."[31] That community exists in this world as an embodiment of Christ's lordship, an outpost of the coming future and a witness to the reconciliation God intends for all. It is a divine creation in danger of being subverted by the inability to live peaceably with disagreements, which is why Paul urges his readers, "Do not, for the sake of food, destroy the work of God" (14:20).

This is the big picture we are likely to lose sight of when mired in church conflict: our participation, by divine grace at work among us, in the cosmic, reconciling purposes of God—our corporate witness to the future God has in mind for the whole creation. But in times of myopic forgetfulness, Scripture serves to "re-mind" us and bring us back to what we should already know,[32] and so Paul's discussion climaxes with an outpouring of quotations (15:7–13). He draws on a full range of Old Testament voices—from the Pentateuch, Prophets, and Psalms[33]—to remind his readers of God's plan from the very beginning to unite all peoples in Jesus Christ. That plan unfolded in the covenant life of the people Israel and was brought to its climax in Israel's Messiah, Jesus Christ, who opened the way for Gentiles to rejoice in God's mercy. Only here at the tail end of the discussion are specific ethnic labels employed, as Paul projects the big picture onto the screen, recalling Christ's service to both Jews and Gentiles and reminding those wrestling with ethnic tensions in Rome that their destinies are intertwined.

Now it becomes clear why the matter of living with disagreements faithfully is such an important one for Paul, requiring extended discussion, and why the conflict among Roman Christians was in danger of subverting the gospel in his view. Much was at stake: the unity of humankind, for which Christ died and for which God raised him—a unity visibly embodied in the community of those who acknowledge God's gracious lordship in Christ.[34] Maintaining Christian unity, then, "is not just a matter of preventing squabbles and bad feeling in the church," says Wright. "It is part of essential Christian witness to the one Lord."[35] Robert Jewett eloquently puts it this way: by living more faithfully with their disagreements, "the Christians in Rome will be enabled to join their voices in praise of the same God (15:6) and to participate credibly in augmenting the global chorus that will one day unite the warring world (15:9–13)."[36]

The credibility of our witness, too, is at stake as we engage differences and disagreements that are no less painful to us than they were to the Christians in first-century Rome. Differences are not likely to disappear, and disagreements are not always resolved— nor do they always need to be, for Paul's discussion presumes that differences have a place in the church, that subgroup identities are not erased, and that a Christian community "should be able to sustain a diversity of opinion and lifestyle as an integral aspect of its common life," as Dunn observes.[37] Indeed, says Dunn, Paul recognizes that "the richness of Christian truth and its expression could allow a range of views and lifestyles and all be legitimate, strongly held in good faith."[38] So he does not attempt to dispel diversity. Instead, he prays for harmony within diversity and exhorts his readers to live more faithfully with their differences and disagreements—not just for their own sake, but for the sake of the world.

"Welcome one another, therefore, just as Christ has welcomed you, for the glory of God" (15:7). As Richard Hays observes, "This same urgent exhortation comes to us in our time." But note:

> We are called to welcome one another, despite our pain-inflicting differences, not because we believe in "tolerance" or "inclusiveness" or individual rights. No, we are called to welcome one another because we have been claimed by Jesus Christ, who has welcomed us into his family. It may be a turbulent family—but it shapes our identity in ways we cannot escape. And our celebration together is a sign and foretaste of the celebration that all creation will offer at the end: "As I live, says the Lord, every knee shall bow to me and every tongue shall confess to God" (14:11, echoing Isa 45:23).[39]

One final observation bearing on the credibility of our witness needs pondering if ever we are tempted to turn our backs on conflict and walk away from those with whom we differ—if ever we are tempted to pick up our toys and play elsewhere, with our own kind, who are always more appealing company. It is how the world around us far too often deals with differences and conflict—that is, with denial, with withdrawal and segregation, and sometimes tragically, with violence. Thus, it should not escape our attention that the community to whom the text was first addressed was living in the capital city of the Roman Empire and that, as N.T. Wright observes, Paul was interested in maintaining communities united in loyalty to Jesus as Lord, right under Caesar's nose:

> A church that all too obviously embodies the social, ethnic, cultural, and political divisions of its surrounding world is no

real challenge to the Caesars of this world. It is only when representatives of many nations worship the world's true Lord in unity that Caesar might get the hint that there is after all "another king." . . . To settle for comfortable disunity because that way we can "be ourselves" and keep things the way we have always known them is to court disloyalty to the one Lord and failure in the church's mission to challenge the gospel of Caesar with the gospel of Jesus Christ.[40]

If we believe that Jesus is Lord, and Caesar is not, the challenge before us is learning to live more faithfully with our own disagreements, that he may be glorified—thereby embracing our role in God's plan for the world's blessing.

QUESTIONS FOR DISCUSSION OR REFLECTION

Begin by reading aloud Romans 14:1–15:13. Pause to collect your first impressions of the text and, if you are engaged in group study, to share them with others. What strikes you most about this text? What questions does it raise for you?

The text contains a great deal of repeated language. What are some of the concepts that are underlined by way of repetition? What words strike you as particularly important as you think about the language Paul is using in this text?

What labels do you imagine the "weak" might have used to describe the "strong"? If you are currently in the midst of church conflict, what are some of the descriptive labels you have used to describe your "opponents," and what are some of the labels they have used to describe you? What impact do you think these epithets have on your relationship?

Paul is very concerned about attitudes Christians harbor toward each other. How would you summarize the attitudinal adjustment he calls for? Would you agree with

James Dunn that the attitudes of "judging" and "despising" reflect a perennial clash between two fundamentals—that of constitutive tradition and practice on the one hand, and that of liberty of faith in Christ on the other? Does this observation illumine your experience of church conflict in any way? If so, how? When you find yourself in the midst of church conflict, is your own attitudinal tendency toward judging or despising?

What do you think of Paul's contention that we will be just as accountable to God for our *attitudes* toward brothers and sisters in Christ with whom we disagree as we will be for the *decisions* we have made that divide us from one another?

What similarities do you discern between the ancient church conflict in Rome between the "strong" and the "weak" and conflict in which your congregation or denomination may be engaged? What differences strike you?

Share your reactions to this observation of N. T. Wright:

Paul's main point in Romans 14 is that there are some things that appear to divide Christians very deeply in terms of their practice but are, in fact, . . . "things indifferent" that should not be allowed to divide them. Most Christians would agree that there are such "indifferent" matters, but the difficulty is that there is no agreement on what those matters are, and on which matters are so centrally important that to disagree on them means dividing the church.[41]

At present, what matters are at the heart of disagreements within your own church community or denomination? Are these matters ultimately "things indifferent" that should not be allowed to divide you, in your view? Why or why not? Do you believe that being right is not the most important thing?

How willing are you to tolerate different lifestyles within your Christian community?

As Dietrich Bonhoeffer observes, the Bible speaks with remarkable frequency of "bearing": "It is capable of expressing the whole work of Jesus Christ in this one word. 'Surely he hath borne our griefs, and carried our sorrows . . . the chastisement of our peace was upon him' (Isa. 53:4–5)." He notes that "bearing" can also characterize the whole life of the Christian, for disciples are to bear both the cross and the burden of other members of the Christian fellowship. Examine some of the other New Testament texts that speak of this "ministry of bearing" in relation to fellow Christians and articulate your response to them (see Gal. 6:1–2; Col. 3:12–17; Eph. 4:1–6; also see 1 Cor. 13:7). You may also want to consider the following observations from Bonhoeffer's discussion of the ministry of bearing in *Life Together* and reflect upon them:

It is, first of all, the freedom of the other person . . . that is a burden to the Christian. The other's freedom collides with his own autonomy, yet he must recognize it. He could get rid of this burden by refusing the other person his freedom, by constraining him and thus doing violence to his personality, by stamping his own image upon him. But if he lets God create His image in him, he by this token gives him his freedom and himself bears the burden of this freedom of another creature of God. The freedom of the other person includes all that we mean by a person's nature, individuality, endowment. It also includes his weaknesses and oddities, which are such a trial to our patience, everything that produces frictions, conflicts, and collisions among us. To bear the burden of the other person means involvement with the created reality of the other, to accept and affirm it, and, in bearing with it, to break through to the point where we take joy in it. This will prove especially difficult where varying strength and weakness in faith are bound together in a fellowship.[42]

Luke Timothy Johnson points out that in Romans 14–15 Paul engages an issue that today is referred to as "multiculturalism":

How can people share a certain unifying community identity without having to lose completely their particular cultural heritage? What differences divide and disable the community, and which ones should be celebrated as enriching it? How much diversity can a specific community tolerate before it disintegrates? And how can the community discern which practices are essential to its life and which ones are not?[43]

> What do these observations contribute to your reflection on the text and its significance for the life of the church? How is multicultural reality reflected in the life of your congregation or denomination? What challenges has it presented?
>
> Romans 14–15 can be misinterpreted as a warrant for moral free agency. Consider this important observation by Richard Hays and share your reaction to it:

Because Paul counsels mutual acceptance of differing views in the church, this passage has become a favorite proof text for advocates of tolerance and inclusivity. It certainly does look as though Paul is saying that everybody has a right to his or her own opinion. . . . Romans 14 looks at first glance like a charter for us all to do what is right in our own eyes. But if we read this passage and find only a message about "tolerance" and the sanctity of individual conscience, we have gravely misunderstood the foundation on which Paul's argument is built.

In the laissez-faire free-market individualism that has enveloped the mainline Protestant church I grew up in, we believe that we should tolerate diversity because individual "choice" is sacred in itself and because we really don't believe that God judges anybody. God *affirms* everybody and everything. Because God doesn't judge, we shouldn't either. So the word "God" describes a great foggy cloud of benevolent indifference. . . .

But Paul's account of the matter is very different: the reason we are not to judge each other is not because God doesn't judge us; rather, it is because God *will* judge us. We are not moral free agents; rather, each of us is God's servant, and we will be called upon to present a detailed account to

the One who is our Lord and master. We should be concerning ourselves with that, not with judging a servant who
does not belong to us.[44]

How do you respond to N. T. Wright's observation on the
    closing page of this chapter: "A church that all too obvi-
    ously embodies the social, ethnic, cultural, and political
    divisions of its surrounding world is no real challenge to
    the Caesars of this world"?
What new insights have emerged from your engagement
    with Romans 14–15 and discussion of it? What ques-
    tions linger?

4

Testing the Spirits I

Jeremiah 28

Struggle, confrontation, and conflict are inescapable in the life of the church as believers, guided by Scripture, seek to discern and embody the will of God and the implications of the gospel in changing times and places. That discernment is challenging and requires engagement with often varied, even conflicting, interpretations of Scripture and, consequently, differing conclusions about what God is calling us to be and do. Thus, strange as it may seem, the church has done some of its best theological reflection in the midst of conflict, which has often proved to be the arena of God's guidance and activity among us. Indeed, as we noted in chapter 1, Karl Barth urged that we not spare ourselves "relative conflict," for only as we wrestle with our varied readings of Scripture will we discern what form Christ is taking among us here and now.

Believers rely on the guidance of the Holy Spirit as they engage in that holy wrestling—with both the Bible and each other. The New Testament presents the Holy Spirit as a gift of God to the Christian community and presupposes that all believers are Spirit-filled. The problem, of course, is that we do not always agree about the Spirit's leading! And what are we to

do when we find ourselves in conflict over our discernment of
the will and work of God? Sometimes we are able to live with
the communal tension of multiple interpretations, but in some
cases we can't all be right—some of us have to be wrong! And
how do we tell? Both the Old Testament and the New Testament grapple with this question of discernment—of "testing
the spirits"—and in this chapter and the next we will consider
key texts from each to see if they provide criteria or norms that
might inform our own holy wrestling.

In the Old Testament, we find an ongoing debate over the test
of true and false prophets. Jeremiah, more than anyone else in
the Old Testament, agonizes over rival readings of historical realities, each of which claims to represent the will and work of
God.[1] Jeremiah 28, the classic account of conflict between true
and false prophecy, has had more attention than any other chapter in the Old Testament in relation to questions about discernment and criteria for distinguishing between true and false words
from the Lord, and thus it begs for our attention. Prophets, after
all, were not primarily in the business of predicting the future,
but of exhorting believers to remain faithful to God.[2] We too
enter into discernment of God's will and work in our time and
place in order that we may respond faithfully to it, so this ancient
prophetic struggle is quite relevant to our concerns.

It is important to attend to the context of the story in Jeremiah 28 as we engage it. The historical context is one of major
geopolitical upheaval in the ancient Near East. Assyria is on the
wane, and the Babylonian Empire is on the rise. We need here
to note two important dates: 598 and 587 BCE. Babylon
attacked Judah in 598, and then again, in devastating fashion,
in 587, the year that marked the great crisis of Israel's history—
the destruction of the temple and the exile of God's people.
Jeremiah 28 is located *between* these two dates during the reign
of Zedekiah, just after the first incursion of Babylonians into
Jerusalem. The first wave of Jewish exiles has been carried away,
and the controversy engaged in Jeremiah 28 concerns how long
the exile will last—how long Yahweh will permit Babylon to
exercise sovereignty over Jerusalem and its citizens.[3]

Literary context is also important, for chapters 27 and 28 are closely related. Chapter 27 begins with a dramatic action on the part of the prophet Jeremiah, who takes a yoke, worn by oxen, and straps it to his neck. He does this to symbolize the political submission of Judah to Babylon. Moreover, he insists that the yoke of Babylon is worn at Yahweh's command—not Nebuchadnezzar's—for astonishingly, Jeremiah speaks of Nebuchadnezzar as God's servant (27:6).[4] The rest of chapter 27 is a long speech explaining this striking act, in which Jeremiah makes four major points that Patrick D. Miller helpfully summarizes: (1) The Lord of Israel is in control of history. (2) At this point in time and history, the Lord is giving the nations, including Judah, over to Babylon. It is Yahweh's direct intent and should not be challenged or resisted by the nations. (3) You are going to have to "serve" the king of Babylon. Failure to submit will lead to an even worse fate—total destruction. (4) Do not let false prophets seduce you into imagining a third alternative—resistance to the empire or miraculous rescue—for this is fantasy, massive denial.[5] Jeremiah would agree with those prophets that the exile will not last forever, but it will last for a long time. God will restore Judah to its land, but not anytime soon. Things are going to get a lot worse before there is a change in Judah's fortunes, for restoration does not negate exile. Prophecies of a future without judgment are lies.[6] Thus, a key difference between the messages of Jeremiah and these false prophets concerns the matter of timing.[7]

Chapter 28 then features a dramatic confrontation reflecting this dispute. It is the most direct, dramatic encounter between opposing prophets in the Old Testament, both of whom claim to be speaking the word of God. They present alternative visions, even contradictory interpretations, of Judah's crisis and of what God is doing in their time, so it is an encounter that invites us to ponder how to distinguish among those who speak for God but do so in conflicting ways. The confrontation takes place in a very public forum, the temple courts, before a live audience. Jeremiah is still wearing the yoke that God commanded him to wear.

I recommend that you stop at this point and read Jeremiah's account of this confrontation. If you are engaged in group study, do a dramatic reading: assign roles to a narrator, to Jeremiah, and to Hananiah. Ask the rest of the group to represent the people overhearing this exchange. Then gather first impressions: What strikes you most as you hear this story? What questions does it raise for you? If you had been present on this occasion, what do you imagine your own reaction to these two very different prophecies would have been?

Hananiah presents what must surely have been the more appealing prospect, the more optimistic version of Judah's future: the Babylonian problem, a temporary setback, will soon be behind them! Just two more years, and those deported to Babylon will be back home. The implements and vessels of the temple will be recovered, the exiled Davidic king, Jeconiah, will be back upon his throne, and life in Jerusalem will return to normal. In fact, Jeremiah's first response to Hananiah is "Amen"—he seems to wish that it were so! He derives no joy from his responsibility as bearer of bad tidings. But he can't shake the sense that, as Walter Brueggemann puts it, Hananiah is a bit "soft on the dangers of covenant disobedience" and that "there are no 'quick fixes' for a people which distorts Yahweh's will."[8] Judah stands at a defining moment in its history and must embrace the wrenching experience of exile before any future is possible.[9] In fact, in the very next chapter (Jer. 29) Jeremiah writes a pastoral letter to those refugees in Babylon, advising them that they might as well unpack! Settle down, he says. Build houses. Plant gardens. Put down roots. You're going to be there a good long while, but the transforming hand and hope of God will be at work in the community that forms amid the suffering of exile.

Imagine being in the shoes of those who witnessed this dramatic prophetic face-off. The live audience no doubt included well-meaning folk with honest concern for the community—people who genuinely wanted to discern God's will for them in the midst of rapidly shifting circumstances and who were painfully aware that real and dangerous policy decisions and consequences were at stake. Both prophets spoke earnestly, but both could hardly be right. One of them had to be wrong, tragically so. And would it not have been exceedingly difficult to discern which of the two spoke the authentic word from God? We have the benefit of hindsight, of course, and know that Jeremiah won this showdown in the end. But would this have been obvious to those who witnessed this confrontation and whose well-being depended on proper discernment?

The story suggests that discernment is exceedingly difficult, for one of the most striking things about the encounter is how very similar Hananiah and Jeremiah are in many ways. Both are models of prophetic propriety.[10] Like Jeremiah, Hananiah is credentialed, given genealogical and geographical identity ("the prophet Hananiah son of Azzur, from Gibeon," v. 1). They speak in similar fashion, both utilizing the standard conventions of prophetic discourse—a "messenger formula" that identifies their word as from God ("thus says the Lord of hosts, the God of Israel," vv. 2, 11, 13–14, 16). And they both engage in dramatic prophetic acts: Jeremiah by strapping the ox yoke to his neck, and Hananiah by taking it from him and breaking it. Moreover, though Jeremiah points out that Hananiah's prophecy is not in the mainstream, it is by no means unorthodox. Indeed, it is grounded in Israel's covenantal theology and stands in the tradition of Isaiah, who a century earlier had prophesied God's deliverance of Jerusalem from Assyria, convinced that Zion would never fall.[11] Nor can it be said that Hananiah speaks as a huckster, pandering to the crowd, telling them exactly what they want to hear; his prophecy, too, is risky. Zedekiah, the current occupant of the throne, may not warm to the news that the exiled King Jeconiah will soon return to Jerusalem to displace him. And how will the Babylonian overlords receive the news that their sovereignty over Judah is about to come to an end? (As one commentator avers, it is small wonder that Hananiah is dead by the end of this story.)[12] In short, Hananiah is presented as one who meets standards of prophetic protocol and acts in good faith; there is no reason to doubt his conviction that he speaks God's word.[13] Jeremiah does not question his sincerity or impugn his integrity;[14] it is not the man but the *message* that he deems false. But initially even Jeremiah seems flummoxed, unsure how to respond when Hananiah takes the yoke from his neck and breaks it, for their first encounter ends on a strange note: "At this, the prophet Jeremiah went his way" (28:11).

What do you make of this odd departure? (Many commentators note that Jeremiah's restraint and dignity throughout his initial engagement with Hananiah is somewhat out of character, given his penchant for denunciation. He is rarely reluctant to heap abuse upon the heads of others.) How would you interpret this action? Perhaps in this instance Jeremiah models for us a wise response in the midst of difficult discernment, creating time and space for careful reflection and patient waiting upon a clear word from God, fully aware that discernment is not immediate or easily attained. Carol Bechtel, for example, finds Jeremiah's reaction "very telling":

> Until his words are vindicated by God through history, or until he receives another word from the Lord that contradicts Hananiah's, he cannot be sure whose position is right. For all he knows, Hananiah may have a genuine word from the Lord. In the meantime, Jeremiah is free only to argue his position and point out the probabilities. Even when his adversary resorts to humiliation and violence (Hananiah actually takes the yoke from Jeremiah's neck and breaks it), Jeremiah does not respond in kind. In what has to be one of the most frustrating phrases in Scripture, Jeremiah 28:11 says, "At this, the prophet Jeremiah went his way."
>
> Most of us do not receive direct revelations from God in the same way that the Old Testament prophets did. Moreover, many of our disputes are not so neatly depicted in black and white. Yet something can be learned from Jeremiah's demeanor in the story. The next time we square off—especially with another believer—we would do well to remember Jeremiah's refusal to claim a corner on the truth. Who knows? God may be speaking to our adversary too. Until we know for sure, perhaps the best we can do is to argue our case and simply walk away. Truth—like murder—will out.[15]

When a clear word from God does, eventually, come to him and he arrives at a more accurate interpretation of God's demand, Jeremiah returns to relay it. The wooden yoke will be replaced with one of iron that cannot be broken, which is to say that the people of Judah will indeed serve King Nebuchadnezzar of Babylon, and for a good long while. He also declares Hananiah as one whom God has *not* sent in this particular instance and who will be dead within a year, because he spoke "rebellion against the Lord" and "made this people trust in a lie" (28:15–16). Hananiah does in fact die within the year—a sobering ending to the story. Interestingly, we are not told that it was *God* who destroyed him. But perhaps we are given to understand that religious leaders will be held accountable for misrepresentation of the word and work of God.

Can this strange story inform our own wrestling with discernment as we test the spirits, engaging conflicting interpretations of Scripture and differing conclusions about what God is calling us to be and do? It could be argued that *they* had it easy, for our own conflicts would be resolved expeditiously if those who were *wrong* would just *drop dead*.[16] But as this is unlikely, does the story set forth any rudimentary norms for distinguishing between true and false prophecy, for discerning whose interpretation is truly from God? Two explicit norms at least, articulated in verses 8–9, are worth pondering.

RECEIVED TRADITION AND PARTICULAR HISTORICAL MOMENTS

The first norm is the *received tradition*, for Jeremiah urges attention to what past prophets have said: "The prophets who preceded you and me from ancient times prophesied war, famine, and pestilence against many countries and great kingdoms" (28:8). For the most part, God's prophets have announced judgment rather than grace, so Hananiah is noted as an exception to the norm, as one who argues against the mainstream. He is suspect because he does not say what prophets characteristically say.

This first norm is not infallible, for prophets of the past spoke oracles of salvation or peace (for example, Isaiah, whose prophecy may well have had an influence on Hananiah). So this norm is a statement of likelihood. But as Patrick Miller notes, the suggestion is that "if we keep reading and listening to the prophetic voices of Scripture . . . we may have the resources at hand for discerning the voices of those who are 'truly sent' in our own time."[17] Surely our own discernment should be informed by the tradition, especially by careful attention to Scripture, but also by attention to wisdom of the past embodied in the church's creeds and confessions—wisdom that has stood the test of time.

But tradition is never static and must constantly be reinterpreted in new times and places. As we saw in chapter 1, Scripture is a living word through which God continues to meet us and speak to us in our own particular historical moment, and thus it demands to be newly interpreted for new historical situations. Moreover, interpretation is not simply reiteration of the text, but the hard work of bringing it into our own time and place; the same is true of the church's engagement with other media of tradition. Thomas Overholt identifies this as Hananiah's misstep: failure to discern Yahweh's will for a particular historical moment. As he points out, "The curious thing is that considered apart from its historical context, there is nothing particularly 'false' about Hananiah's message," grounded as it is in covenantal theology, but Hananiah misreads Israel's election faith:

> It is certainly true that Yahweh has chosen this people and wills their salvation (cf. Deut. 7:6ff., 20:4), but Hananiah had apparently forgotten that the covenant also carries with it definite obligations which the people must fulfill. He apparently failed to interpret the political events of his day as a punishment leveled by Yahweh against a sinful people. Instead, he applied an *old* message in a *new* situation, and thus demonstrated an "*inability to orient himself in the new historical situation,* viz. to perceive the will of God for a specific situation and at a specific place."[18]

Louis Stulman draws the same conclusion: "Hananiah adequately recites the tradition, yet without using critical lenses to address the current crisis of the community. Although he speaks out of the authoritative traditions of ancient Israel, he is out of touch with the political and spiritual subtleties of his moment in history." His message thereby obscures the danger threatening Judah. Jeremiah, by contrast, painfully "sensitive to the people's recalcitrance (2:20–22; 13:20–27) was able to interpret the present destructive course of events as nothing other than the negative activity of a God who now found it necessary to punish his sinful people."[19]

What is the upshot for our own engagement with discernment? Overholt penned these words forty years ago, but they are still germane: "The times in which we live are, indeed, rapidly changing. Perhaps more than ever before the solutions of a past generation to the problems of obedient existence cannot simply be taken over as our solutions."[20] It is surely incumbent on us, as it was on ancient prophets, to discern and articulate God's will in terms appropriate to the concrete historical situation in which we find ourselves. This will require careful dual attention on our parts, both to the received tradition—the wisdom of the past that has stood the test of time—and also to the particular historical circumstances in which we live.

Overholt's observations resonate with those of Patrick Miller and Walter Brueggemann, both of whom draw attention to the striking relation between theology and politics in the prophecy of Jeremiah. Their observations also warrant consideration:

> Theology and politics are once again joined in the prophecy of Jeremiah. . . . There is an awareness that the realm of God's work in the world is the affairs of people and nations, the politics of alliances and the rise and fall of empires. . . . What is going on in history is fraught with human decisions, inclinations, evil, and good. It is all the context in which the Lord is working out the divine purposes, a context that itself is provided by the Creator. The politics of

human communities are found to be in some fashion coterminus with the politics of God. That is not something we can always discern or make sense of, and there may be times when we have to call human evil simply that and make no more of it. But Jeremiah suggests that we think about what is going on in the world as God's work, even with alien and strange instruments.[21] (Miller)

The issue of truth and falsehood in theological discernment is not, in the book of Jeremiah, simply a matter of having right information or right discernment. It is, rather, an interpretive issue of recognizing that the transcendent will of Yahweh is completely coherent with socioeconomic, political processes. It is in, with, and under Babylon that God is at work. The falseness of Jeremiah's opponents is not that they did not believe in and trust Yahweh, but that they tried to keep Yahweh apart from the world processes of their time.[22] (Brueggemann)

In light of all this, Karl Barth's famous dictum regarding preaching would appear also to hold true for discernment: it needs to be done "with the Bible in one hand and the newspaper in the other."

WHETHER OR NOT PROPHECY COMES TO PASS

If the first norm articulated in verses 8–9 is the received tradition, reinterpreted in particular historical moments, the second norm is this: whether or not prophecy comes to pass. Jeremiah declares, "As for the prophet who prophesies peace, when the word of that prophet comes true, then it will be known that the Lord has truly sent the prophet" (28:9). The classic statement of this test appears in Deuteronomy 18:21–22: "You may say to yourself, 'How can we recognize a word that the Lord has not spoken?' If a prophet speaks in the name of the Lord but the thing does not take place or prove true, it is a word that the Lord has not spoken. The prophet has spoken it presumptuously; do not be frightened by it." However, lack of success is not a sure sign, as Jeremiah himself notes earlier in 26:18–19. Micah prophesied devastation of Jerusalem and it did not come to pass, for God's mind could "change" about a word of judgment.[23] The prophetic word does not bind God, who is always free to change plans for the covenant people. Deuteronomy also recognizes that false prophecies can be fulfilled. Thus, a more basic criterion is noted in Deuteronomy 13:1–5: *loyalty to Yahweh* ("If prophets . . . say 'Let us follow other gods . . . and let us serve them,' you must not heed the words of those prophets").

This second norm, concerning whether or not prophecy comes to pass, does not help us much in the present, when decisions must be made and policies enacted. The problem we face, says Brueggemann, is that faithful discernment of the will and work of God "must always be done 'in the middle of things,' before the data are all in."[24] But perhaps one last word of wisdom can be gleaned from the story to help us on our way. Commentator John Bracke shares an insight well worth pondering, calling our attention to the often disorienting, unsettling impact of the word of God:

> Understanding the basis of the conflict between Jeremiah and Hananiah may help us with the issue of how we might respond when persons who claim that they speak for God offer very different perspectives. We need to be careful about generalizing from the specific instance presented to us in Jeremiah 28. Like those who witnessed the conflict between Jeremiah and Hananiah, we need to decide in each situation, with all its complexity and uncertainty, who speaks for God. *Still, Jeremiah 28 suggests to us that it is well to be suspicious of those who, like Hananiah, speak words of comfort and reassurance that we want to hear and that are easy for us.* Rather, "from ancient times" (v. 8) the persons more likely to have been sent by God are those whose message is *discomforting and disturbing*—"war, famine, and pestilence"—like the hard words of Jeremiah who announced that God intended a long dominion for Babylon over Judah and the nations. *We, like the people of ancient Judah, are drawn to the assurance of the Hananiahs among us. Jeremiah 28 claims that God is*

more likely to speak to us through the hard words of the Jeremi-
ahs, who announce that God is disrupting and ending the
world in which we are so comfortable.[25]

Perhaps, then, we should exercise caution when our perception
of the authentic word from God is suspiciously close to the
word we most want to hear, or when those who claim to speak
for God convey only words of comfort and peace.[26]

Engagement with Jeremiah's dramatic face-off with Hananiah leaves us without surefire criteria for discernment in hand,
but with guideposts by which to make our way and perhaps
with greater awareness of just how challenging—and urgent—
the testing of spirits can be. The early church continued to
wrestle with this issue, and it is to the New Testament that we
turn now.

QUESTIONS FOR DISCUSSION AND REFLECTION

If you are engaged in group study, begin with a dramatic reading of Jeremiah 28. Assign roles to a narrator, to Jeremiah,
and to Hananiah. Ask the rest of the group to represent the
people overhearing this exchange. Then gather first impressions: What strikes you most as you hear this story? What
questions does it raise for you? If you had been present on
this occasion, what do you imagine your own evaluation of
the two very different prophecies would have been?

The prophets Hananiah and Jeremiah are similar in
many ways. What similarities catch your attention? What
differences?

How do you interpret Jeremiah's response in verse 6
("Amen! May the LORD do so; may the LORD fulfill the
words that you have prophesied")? What do you imagine
the tone of his voice to have been? Is he bemused? Sarcas-
tic or mocking? Anguished? Is he saying he is open to this
possibility, or that his own wish and hope is for this positive outcome?

What do you make of Jeremiah's puzzling response in verse 11: "At this, the prophet Jeremiah went his way"? How would you interpret this action? Do you find Jeremiah's demeanor in verses 6 and 11 to be instructive for your own engagement in discernment and conflict it evokes? If so, how?

How does the story suggest we should go about distinguishing between true and false prophecy? What rudimentary norms for discernment does it present? Which do you find most helpful, and why?

Consider Jeremiah 27:16–22, Jeremiah's taunting of false prophets, where a final norm for discernment can be observed: true prophets engage in intercession for the community. As Patrick Miller notes, "The prophet was the intercessor *par excellence* in ancient Israel. The absence of intercession marks these prophets as truly not knowing what is going on, not knowing what time it really is."[27] Is this a helpful criterion, in your view?

What would you identify as Hananiah's misstep or fatal flaw? Would you agree with Overholt's assessment of it as failure to discern Yahweh's will for a particular historical moment? Why or why not?

What connections do you discern between this story and difficult processes of discernment in which your congregation or denomination may currently be engaged?

Revisit Patrick Miller's and Walter Brueggemann's observations on pages 61–62 and share your reactions to them, as well as your own thoughts on the striking connection between theology and politics in this story.

Revisit John Bracke's observations on pages 63–64 about the disorienting, unsettling impact of the word of God and share your reaction to them. What implications do they bear for your own engagement with discernment?

What new insights have emerged for you from your reflection on this story? What questions linger?

5

Testing the Spirits II

1 Corinthians 12–14

It is clear from a reading of the New Testament that the early Christians experienced the Holy Spirit as a dynamic presence in their lives. It was for them a sign that the new age had dawned—that in the life, death, and resurrection of Jesus Christ, God had set the future in motion. It was, moreover, a gift of divine power, so to receive it was to walk into the coming age with power. No one received it privately, for it was a gift to the whole community; still, the New Testament presupposes that all who believe in Christ are Spirit-filled.[1]

But it is also clear, says James Dunn, that "when someone spoke under inspiration the community did not simply listen gape-mouthed and accept it without question as a word of the exalted Christ" or a word of God.[2] On the contrary, early Christians were aware of the very real danger of false inspiration, false prophecy, false teaching. Whenever people claimed that the words they spoke were inspired by God's Spirit, there was an accompanying recognition that the claim might be false—that it had to be tested, weighed, and assessed before it could be approved as a word of God. Thus, we encounter in the New Testament the notion of testing the spirits. The earliest document in the New Testament, 1 Thessalonians, for example, advises, "Do not quench the Spirit. Do not despise the words of prophets, but test everything; hold fast to what is good; abstain from every form of evil" (1 Thess. 5:19–22). So how did they go about testing the spirits? Were there norms or criteria for that discernment?

We must turn to the apostle Paul for guidance on this matter, for as Dunn observes, "Of the first generation Christians, it was Paul who . . . grasped most clearly the danger of an inspiration whose source was demonic and whose utterance could not be trusted. Wherever he is confronted with prophecy as a living force he is quick to indicate that prophetic inspiration alone is no guarantee that the inspired word is of the Spirit. So much so that *every* prophetic utterance must be subjected to careful scrutiny and evaluation."[3]

Paul's discussion of prophecy in 1 Corinthians 12–14, the most extensive in the New Testament, is especially relevant to our concerns. He does not provide a precise definition of prophecy in these chapters (he presumes that the Corinthians know what he is talking about), but he does describe its functions: "Those who prophesy speak to other people for their upbuilding and encouragement and consolation" (1 Cor. 14:3). "For you can all prophesy one by one, so that all may learn and all be encouraged" (1 Cor. 14:31). Prophecy, then, seems to be a statement for the community and those in worship that is given to meet needs within the Christian community for edification, encouragement, consolation, learning, guidance, and direction.[4] As in the Old Testament, it is not simply a matter of predicting the future but rather of declaring God's will, speaking on behalf of God to a particular situation of need in the present.[5]

Interestingly, Paul clearly expected that members of the congregation other than recognized prophets could be granted a word of prophecy: "Pursue love and strive for the spiritual gifts, and especially that you may prophesy" (1 Cor. 14:1). "So, my friends, be eager to prophesy, and do not forbid speaking in tongues; but all things should be done decently and in order" (1 Cor. 14:39–40). Moreover, all were involved in the "testing" of any word of prophecy, for discernment of whether or not it represented a word from God was a decidedly communal endeavor. "Prophecy" and "discernment" were thus closely connected. Indeed, note how closely Paul links them in 1 Corinthians 12 and 14:

> Now there are varieties of gifts, but the same Spirit; and there are varieties of services, but the same Lord; and there are varieties of activities, but it is the same God who activates all of them in everyone. To each is given the manifestation of the Spirit for the common good. To one is given through the Spirit the utterance of wisdom, and to another the utterance of knowledge according to the same Spirit, to another faith by the same Spirit, to another gifts of healing by the one Spirit, to another the working of miracles, to another prophecy, to another the discernment of spirits, to another various kinds of tongues, to another the interpretation of tongues. All these are activated by one and the same Spirit, who allots to each one individually just as the Spirit chooses. (1 Cor. 12:4–11)

> Let two or three prophets speak, and let the others weigh what is said. (1 Cor. 14:29)

The Greek words for "discernment" and "weighing" in these verses (the noun *diakrisis* and the verb *diakrinō*) have the connotation of differentiating, distinguishing, judging, evaluating carefully—of recognizing a thing for what it is. Discerning spirits means knowing who is influenced by the Holy Spirit and who is not.

We too need to know this if we are to follow the Spirit's leading in our time and place. According to 1 Corinthians 12:10, discernment of spirits is itself a gift of the Spirit of God. However, Dunn helpfully identifies several norms that surface repeatedly in Paul's discussion of this matter: (1) the test of the gospel, or norm of earlier revelation; (2) the character and conduct of the prophet, or test of love; and (3) the test of community benefit.[6] Each of these norms warrants attention as we engage the challenges of discernment in our own day.

THE TEST OF THE GOSPEL, OR NORM
OF EARLIER REVELATION

In 1 Corinthians 12:3, Paul presents a very clear rule of thumb for evaluating spiritual utterances, a summary confession of the gospel—indeed, its foundational claim: Jesus is Lord! "I want you to understand that no one speaking by the Spirit of God ever says 'Let Jesus be cursed!' and no one can say 'Jesus is Lord' except by the Holy Spirit" (1 Cor. 12:3). We do not know whether the scenario envisioned is hypothetical or real, and speculation abounds. Have Corinthians actually dared to curse Jesus? Some think it likely, perhaps under the influence of proto-gnostic devaluation of the flesh and consequent exaltation of the heavenly Jesus over the earthly one; others speculate that cursing of Jesus might have been coerced under trial or torture; or perhaps the curse represents Jewish rejection of the church's confession of Christ's lordship—even Paul's own assessment of Jesus prior to his conversion, during the period of his life when he persecuted Christians (to mention but a few of the possibilities).[7] Others consider the scenario hypothetical, a "dramatic fiction"[8] or "shock language" designed to elicit a "we know that" response.[9] But whatever the case may be, the point Paul wishes to emphasize is that those inspired by the Holy Spirit will convey this foundational Christian confession—they "will speak and act in ways that glorify the lordship of Jesus."[10] Anyone who denies that lordship can hardly claim inspiration by the Spirit.

The flip side of this criterion is equally important but easy to forget when engaged in ecclesial combat: the confession "Jesus is Lord" unites the church at the most basic level. Therefore, as Richard Hays observes, "in the midst of serious disagreements within the church, we must recognize that all those who share the confession of Jesus' lordship are our brothers and sisters to whom we are bound by the one Spirit."[11] We may not agree with fellow believers, we may consider them misguided, but they are not infidels, for if they acknowledge Christ's lordship, they do so by the power of the Holy Spirit at work within them.

Paul surely does not intend this basic Christian confession to be the only test that arises out of the gospel. The test is framed differently elsewhere. In Galatians, for example, the test that arises out of the gospel is that of Christian liberty rather than Christology (see Gal. 5:1).[12] Here too, Paul placed a great deal of store on a church's initial experience of and response to the gospel, reprimanding the Galatians for turning from the gospel they initially received:

> I am astonished that you are so quickly deserting the one who called you in the grace of Christ and are turning to a different gospel—not that there is another gospel, but there are some who are confusing you and want to pervert the gospel of Christ. But even if we or an angel from heaven should proclaim to you a gospel contrary to what we proclaimed to you, let that one be accursed! As we have said before, so now I repeat, if anyone proclaims to you a gospel contrary to what you received, let that one be accursed! (Gal. 1:6–9)

In the Epistles of John, the same test is framed to address a particular christological conflict in the community. Some appear to maintain that the humanity (or "flesh") of Jesus had no salvific import. To combat this supposition, the author repeatedly emphasizes the church's initial experience of and response to the gospel, what was "from the beginning":

> We declare to you what was from the beginning, what we have heard, what we have seen with our eyes, what we have looked at and touched with our hands, concerning the word of life. (1 John 1:1)

> Let what you heard from the beginning abide in you. If what you heard from the beginning abides in you, then you will abide in the Son and in the Father. (1 John 2:24)

> Beloved, do not believe every spirit, but test the spirits to see whether they are from God; for many false prophets have gone out into the world. By this you know the Spirit

of God: every spirit that confesses that Jesus Christ has
come in the flesh is from God, and every spirit that does not
confess Jesus is not from God. And this is the spirit of the
antichrist, of which you have heard that it is coming; and
now it is already in the world. Little children, you are from
God, and have conquered them; for the one who is in you
is greater than the one who is in the world. They are from
the world; therefore what they say is from the world, and
the world listens to them. We are from God. Whoever
knows God listens to us, and whoever is not from God does
not listen to us. From this we know the spirit of truth and
the spirit of error. (1 John 4:1–6)

As we saw in the previous chapter, the prophet Jeremiah also
directs attention to earlier revelation in his showdown with the
rival prophet Hananiah, urging attention to what past prophets had said (Jer. 28:8). The fact that Hananiah's optimistic
prophecy did not accord with received tradition led Jeremiah to
suspect that it was false. At the end of the Gospel of Matthew,
Jesus himself invokes the norm of earlier revelation when he
commissions his disciples with these words: "Go therefore
and make disciples of all nations, . . . teaching them to obey
everything that I have commanded you" (Matt. 28:19–20).
Matthew's substantial documentation of Jesus' teaching thus
provides a clear norm for discernment between conflicting views
in the Christian community. As Mark Allan Powell explains,
"Anyone who claims to be teaching what Jesus commanded
ought to be teaching material consistent with the record of Jesus'
ministry that Matthew provides."[13] The test of the gospel, or
norm of earlier revelation, recommended by a range of canonical
witnesses surely merits our continued consideration.

THE CHARACTER AND CONDUCT
OF THE PROPHET, OR TEST OF LOVE

The second test is ethical and one of the most important for
Paul: does the prophet manifest love in the exercise of his or her

gift? It is no accident that Paul's famous chapter on love (1 Cor. 13) is situated at the heart of his long discussion of spiritual gifts in 1 Corinthians 12–14. Many, accustomed to hearing it read at marriage services, may think of it as an ode to romantic love, losing sight of the fact that Paul addressed it to a deeply conflicted church to describe the exercise of love that is to characterize life within the Christian community. So that there may be no doubt as to what this way of being and relating entails, he provides a remarkable (and polemical) description, one that specifically enumerates seven positive attributes of love and eight negations of it: "Love is patient; love is kind; love is *not* envious or boastful or arrogant or rude. It does *not* insist on its own way; it is *not* irritable or resentful; it does *not* rejoice in wrongdoing, but rejoices in the truth. It bears all things, believes all things, hopes all things, endures all things" (1 Cor. 13:4–7). The negations of love noted no doubt provide a glimpse of failures in love on exhibit in the Corinthian congregation (and currently showcased in ecclesial conflicts in our own time and place). Love, in Paul's view, is the more excellent way to exercise any and all spiritual gifts, for from his perspective, writes Frederick Dale Bruner, "without it the Christian graces are dis-graced."[14] Believers are therefore exhorted to "pursue love" (14:1)—to *exert* themselves in the practice of it. Paul wants to see within the life of the Christian community a rigorous practice of attitudes and actions that evidence genuine commitment to the well-being of others—even, and perhaps especially, in the midst of church conflict.

The ethical criterion is invoked elsewhere in the New Testament. In Galatians 5, Paul's discussion of the "fruit of the Spirit" corresponds to his ode to love in 1 Corinthians (see Gal. 5:1, 13–26).[15] "Fruit of the Spirit," which includes "love, joy, peace, patience, kindness, generosity, faithfulness, gentleness, and self-control" (5:22–23), are contrasted with "works of the flesh," such as "fornication, impurity, licentiousness, idolatry, sorcery, enmities, strife, jealousy, anger, quarrels, dissensions, factions, envy, drunkenness, carousing, and things like these" (5:19–21). Those who claim that the Spirit inspires them can be expected to manifest fruit consistent with the Spirit's presence in their lives. The Epistle of 1 John makes the practice of love the key criterion for the testing of spirits: "Those who say, 'I love God,' and hate their brothers or sisters, are liars; for those who do not love a brother or sister whom they have seen, cannot love God whom they have not seen" (1 John 4:20; see also vv. 7–12). In short, failure to love invalidates any claim to know God. Jesus himself provides similar counsel: "Beware of false prophets. . . . You will know them by their fruits" (Matt. 7:15–20). Thus, we are given to understand that if anyone claims to be prophesying or teaching the commandments of Jesus but is not living in the manner that Jesus described, then their understanding of Jesus' words must be suspect and their prophesying or teaching cannot be respected (see also Matt. 12:33–37).[16]

The ethical criterion appears in literature that precedes and follows the New Testament as well. The Old Testament prophets Isaiah and Jeremiah, for example, denounce prophets of their own time for drunkenness, adultery, lying, and encouraging immorality in others (see Isa. 28:7; Jer. 23:14). It is also a key criterion in second-century Christian literature such as the *Didache* and the *Shepherd of Hermas*. The *Didache*, for example, a manual of church instruction, highlights the test of conduct: "It is by their conduct that the false prophet and the true prophet can be distinguished" (11:8). *Hermas* provides similar counsel: "Therefore test by his life and his works the man who says that he is moved by the Spirit" (11:16). It would appear that the "test of love" weathered the test of time, providing a trustworthy barometer for discernment for many generations of believers.

THE TEST OF COMMUNITY BENEFIT

The test of community benefit, the clearest of Paul's criteria, surfaces primarily in 1 Corinthians 14, where it is the leading theme, referenced no less than seven times. It is the test of "building up" or "edification" (*oikodomē* in Greek)—one that seals Paul's preference for the gift of prophecy over that of glossolalia (speaking in tongues):

> Pursue love and strive for the spiritual gifts, and especially that you may prophesy. For those who speak in a tongue do not speak to other people but to God; for nobody understands them, since they are speaking mysteries in the Spirit. On the other hand, those who prophesy speak to other people for their upbuilding and encouragement and consolation. Those who speak in a tongue build up themselves, but those who prophesy build up the church. Now I would like all of you to speak in tongues, but even more to prophesy. One who prophesies is greater than one who speaks in tongues, unless someone interprets, so that the church may be built up. (1 Cor. 14:1–5)

In Paul's view, self-edification can never be the Christian's primary goal.[17] It must always take a backseat to edification of the whole community. This test of community benefit also has decidedly evangelistic implications, for as Paul explains, outsiders who wander into the church and overhear unintelligible speaking in tongues are likely to say, "You are out of your mind" (1 Cor. 14:23). But eavesdropping on intelligible prophecy is much more likely to pierce them with truth, disclosing the secrets of their hearts and leading them to bow down before God and worship, declaring, "God is really among you" (1 Cor. 14:22–25). Dunn eloquently summarizes the test of community benefit this way: "Whatever does not build up, whatever word or action destroys the congregation's unity or causes hurt to its members or leaves the outsider merely bewildered, that word or action fails the test of *oikodomē*, and should be ignored or rejected, no matter how inspired, how charismatic it seems to be."[18] Nowhere else in the New Testament is the test of community benefit articulated as clearly as it is in Paul's letters, but its reappearance throughout them attests to its importance in his understanding of life within the Christian community (see Rom. 14:19; 15:2; 2 Cor. 10:8; 12:19; 13:10; Gal. 2:18; 1 Thess. 5:11).

In sum, Paul articulates three useful criteria for the testing of spirits that warrant reflection as we engage the difficult challenge of discernment today. Dunn suggests that "taken together they provide quite a comprehensive yardstick. It should, however, be stressed that as developed by Paul they do not provide any hard or fast rules or rubrics or laws." Indeed, application of these criteria must be carried out "in conscious dependence on the grace of God and the inspiration of the Spirit."[19]

As we pursue our own discernment of the movement of God's Spirit in the world, one final point should not escape us, one that is presupposed throughout the discussion in 1 Corinthians 12–14: Paul's understanding of the church as a community of discourse—of conversation. In chapter 14 alone, the verb "to speak" (*lalein*) appears twenty-four times. As Bruner astutely observes, "It appears in this chapter that Paul sees the highest expression of spiritual gifts in the free, helpful discussion of Christians together and their contribution in thoughtful speech to each other."[20] Total participation is in view: "You can all prophesy one by one, so that all may learn and all be encouraged" (14:31).[21] And care is taken to ensure that everyone has a chance to speak and be heard—that no one monopolizes the conversation. Therefore, members are to speak "in turn," "one by one," and once one has spoken, one must yield the floor to others (14:27, 31). Silence is required when another is speaking (14:30). Indeed, listening is every bit as important as speaking, for "a church plagued by the commotion of competing prophets vying for attention and dominated by conceited members who refuse to listen to what others have been given to say does not testify to the presence of God (14:25)."[22]

Moreover, those who claim to articulate the Spirit's leading among us must be open to assessment, review, and critique. They should expect deliberation, engaged response from the community. Indeed, "an unwillingness to cooperate in the discernment process is itself an indication that something is wrong."[23] In sum, Paul envisions the church as a community of conversation in which all the members wait together on the guidance of the Spirit and all take responsibility for discerning what God is saying to them.[24] Conversation that is thoughtful, respectful, decent, orderly (1 Cor. 14:40), and fully-engaged is essential for the testing of spirits in every time and place and bears witness that the Holy Spirit is at work among us.

But discernment remains a difficult task. In fact, in the midst of his discussion of spiritual gifts in 1 Corinthians 12–14, Paul candidly observes that during the present age "we see in a mirror, dimly" (1 Cor. 13:12). First John also hints at our partial knowledge, acknowledging, "what we will be has not yet been revealed. What we do know is this: when he is revealed, we will be like him" (1 John 3:2). A measure of humility would thus appear to be advised, as we share our deeply held convictions about God's will for the church in our own day.[25] In truth, "we know only in part, and we prophesy only in part" (13:9). Indeed, our prophecies and knowledge, our perceived monopolies on truth, "will come to an end" (13:8). However, "love never ends" (13:8). Our practice of love will endure beyond us as our legacy,[26] for "faith, hope, and love abide, these three; and the greatest of these is love" (13:13).

QUESTIONS FOR DISCUSSION AND REFLECTION

Begin by reading aloud 1 Corinthians 12–14. Pause to collect your first impressions and, if you are engaged in group study, to share them with others. What strikes you most about this text? What questions does it raise for you?

What repeated concepts do you note in 1 Corinthians 12–14? What words strike you as particularly important as you think about the language Paul is using?

Share your reactions to, and any questions about, the three criteria for discernment that Paul articulates: the test of the gospel (or norm of earlier revelation), the test of love (the character and conduct of the prophet), and the test of community benefit. Which strike you as particularly important or helpful? Which do you find most challenging? Which do you find most difficult to apply, and why?

What connections do you find between these three criteria for discernment and conflicts in which your own congregation or denomination may be currently engaged? How might they inform your practice of communal wrestling with the challenge of testing the spirits?

Theologian Hendrikus Berkhof says that "prophecy is the gift of understanding and expressing what the will of God is for a given present situation."[27] Frederick Dale Bruner observes, "Committees often manifest this gift. The sometimes pastoral disparagement of committee meetings could be modified, perhaps, by appreciating that it is often only in committee meetings that the *charismata* ["gifts," as expressions of divine grace] given the church members have the opportunity of expression."[28] Share your reactions to these observations. How do they square with your experience of church committee meetings?

Paul's eloquent description of love in 1 Corinthians 13 is among the most familiar texts in all of Scripture. What has been your experience with these well-known verses? In what contexts have you encountered them? Have you ever read them through the lens of church conflict? What might they contribute to your reflection on (and practice of) love within the Christian community?

Richard Hays reminds us that "love does not mean uncritical acceptance": "Paul's own example of vigorous confrontation of the Corinthians on various issues should demonstrate that point beyond all question! The love that 'rejoices in the truth' may also require us to speak hard truth at times to those whom we love."[29] On what occasions in your own life have you been required to practice or receive this kind of love?

J. Paul Sampley, commenting on 1 Corinthians 13, observes, "If mountains come and go, but love endures; if love is greater even than faith and hope, then not only does our loving endure beyond us but our loving is our enduring legacy as well. Granted, our loving and its legacy can take many forms. If we took it seriously that our loving was our enduring legacy, then what reorganization would be needed in our lives, in our stewardship of our time, energy, and resources to honor and maximize that legacy?"[30] How would you respond to his observation and question?

Do you experience your congregation or denomination as a healthy community of conversation? In your experience, what practices promote thoughtful, respectful, fully engaged ecclesial conversation? What practices impede it?

What new insights have emerged from your engagement with 1 Corinthians 12–14 and your discussion with each other? What questions linger?

Let Paul have the last word: read his admonition in 2 Corinthians 13:5 and share your reaction to it. What might this final word contribute to our collective discernment if we were to take it to heart?

6

Conflict over Qualifications for Church Leadership

1 Timothy 3:1–16 and 5:17–25

Many mainline denominations are currently embroiled in conflict over qualifications—and disqualifications—for church leadership. Who is qualified or disqualified for service as a church officer, as a minister of the Word and Sacrament, or as a bishop? Early churches also wrestled with this matter, and perhaps a glimpse of their struggle and discernment process can illumine our own. Thus, let me direct your attention to another group of little letters that tend to get few visitors: the Pastoral Epistles, which include 1 and 2 Timothy and Titus. These letters are "pastoral" in the sense that they counsel us how to care for the church,[1] and they have more to say about church leaders than any other New Testament document. Not only do they mention several types of church leaders; they also delineate their qualifications, specifying what makes for a suitable candidate.

Indeed, the Pastoral Epistles provide a fascinating snapshot of a transition moment in the early church: the transition from movement to organization.[2] The second coming of Jesus turned out not to be imminent, and second-generation Christians found themselves constrained to think about the shape of the church's ongoing life. So in these texts we see several distinct functions emerging: those of the *episkopos*, *diakonos*, and *presbyteros* (translated respectively as "bishop," "deacon," and "elder" in the NRSV). The words themselves provide the best clues as to what role or function such persons were playing.

"Bishop" may not be the best translation of *episkopos*, since functions rather than offices are probably in view at this early point in the church's life. The verb *episkopeō* means to "look at" or "to oversee," so *episkopos* implies an overseeing function— someone who keeps an eye on things.[3] *Episkopos*, then, can be translated more literally as "overseer" (as in the NIV) or "superintendent," and these are preferable translations. The *episkopos*, a vigilant supervisor, watches over others to ensure that things are going smoothly.[4] This word was used widely in the Greco-Roman world to refer to persons in positions of general oversight, so it was a natural term to apply to those who exercised leadership roles in emerging Christian churches. It does not correspond to what we today understand by "bishop"—that is, one who is in charge of churches and clergy within a circumscribed geographical area. The notion of a monarchic bishop appears for the first time in Christian literature in the second-century letters of Bishop Ignatius of Antioch.

At the time the Pastoral Epistles were written, an overseer/bishop may have been the supervisor of a particular congregation. The word surfaces for the first time in the New Testament in Philippians 1:1, where Paul greets overseers/bishops (plural) and deacons (plural) in Philippi. Thus, it appears that there were several *episkopoi* in the church at Philippi. Some of us may belong to denominations that have always had an allergic reaction to the notion of a "bishop," but the function of oversight is still very important to us. Presbyterians, for example, choose to exercise that function collectively. Thus, within Presbyterian polity, "presbyteries" (which consist of all the churches and ministers of the Word and Sacrament within a certain district) function as corporate bishops, and within them particular committees (such as the Committee on Ministry and the

Committee on Preparation for Ministry) play special roles in the oversight of ministerial leadership.

The noun *episkopos*, or "overseer," appears only five times in the New Testament (Acts 20:28; Phil. 1:1; 1 Tim. 3:2; Titus 1:7; 1 Pet. 2:25), and in several of those instances it is clearly interchangeable with the second term, *presbyteros*, or "elder." In Titus 1:5–7 and Acts 20:28, for example, the two terms seem to be used synonymously. So there was overlap between overseers and elders, and it is hard to sort out the relationship between them. Overseers appear to have been elders and were probably drawn from this group, though not all elders were overseers. In some instances the word "elders" points simply to senior members of the Christian community (e.g., Titus 2:2). Older persons would have been an obvious pool of leadership, given the accumulated wisdom of age. At points where persons of a particular status are in view, the term "elder" implies someone chosen for his maturity and leadership qualities. In 1 Timothy 5:17, the verb associated with the function of elders is that of "ruling" (thus Presbyterians speak of "ruling elders"). The NIV conveys the ruling function in an alternate translation: elders "direct the affairs of the church well." Thus the word "elder" (*presbyteros*) apparently designates the ruling/directing/ presiding function of a mature, experienced leader, while the *episkopos* has an overseeing function (with overlap between the two).[5] A very fluid pattern of ministry is in view. First Timothy 5 also speaks of some within the circle of elders who have special responsibility for preaching and teaching, and it provides an interesting discussion of remuneration owed that group. (Interestingly, 1 Timothy 5 does not articulate specific qualifications for elders along the lines of those provided for overseers/bishops and deacons in 1 Timothy 3. This may be because qualifications of the elder coincide with those of overseers/bishops and have already been delineated.)

The third function mentioned in the Pastoral Epistles is that of the *diakonos*, or "deacon" (NRSV). The verb *diakoneō* means "to serve," so the function described is that of service (though

1 Timothy does not specify the nature of it). Some, in fact, prefer the translation "server." This flexible word was applied widely to varied tasks and functions. As Jouette Bassler notes, the root idea is that of a "go-between." Thus the *diakonos* "came to signify one who performed acts for, or in service of, another."[6] In sum, three types of church leaders emerge into view in the Pastoral Epistles: overseers/bishops, elders, and servers/deacons, each of whom performed distinct functions in the life of the early church.

A few other words by way of introduction are in order before turning to these letters. The authorship of the Pastoral Epistles is debated. They are attributed to the apostle Paul, but most scholars regard them as pseudonymous letters, which is to say that they were written in Paul's name well after his death by someone who honored his legacy and sought to interpret and apply it to a new time and place. There are very good reasons for thinking that Paul himself did not write them, but we do not need to engage those arguments or even agree about that, as this matter will not bear significantly on a reading of the texts before us. Even if the author is writing under a pseudonym, the concrete reality presented in the letters is not fictitious. As Elsa Tamez emphasizes, a community existed and presented the problems and conflicts that we find in the letters[7]—problems and conflicts that were quite real to those who faced them. Moreover, whether or not Paul wrote these letters, they are still part of the canon of sacred Scripture and thus deserving of our careful attention. However, there is one thing I can venture to say with real confidence: I am quite certain that the Pastoral Epistles were written by a man. Consider 1 Timothy 2:11–12, for example: "Let a woman learn in silence with full submission. I permit no woman to teach or to have authority over a man; she is to keep silent." The author goes on to opine that women are to earn their salvation by bearing children (1 Tim. 2:15). So much for justification by grace through faith alone!

Another debated matter we can sidestep is the identity of the opponents or false teachers referred to in the letter. The author is quite concerned about them, but his attacks on them are vague and imprecise, on the order of name-calling, insults, broadsides, and conventional vilification. Thus it is hard to say what, exactly, their deviant teaching and behavior entailed. The author discredits, rather than describes, his opponents and their teaching. However, it is quite clear that a genuine crisis in leadership is in view.[8] Lewis Donelson puts it this way: the author "perceived his church as being in theological and social disarray. He wants order."[9] Indeed, a major goal of 1 Timothy is to exhort the community and its leaders to embrace certain modes of behavior and avoid others. We see this in 1 Timothy 3:14–15, which provides the purpose statement for the whole letter: "I hope to come to you soon, but I am writing these instructions to you so that, if I am delayed, you may know how one ought to behave in the household of God, which is the church of the living God, the pillar and bulwark of the truth." This purpose statement also presents the central image of the church in the Pastoral Epistles: it is the "household of God."

One last thing is very important to keep in mind as we read these letters—namely, the important difference between prescriptive and descriptive literature.[10] The texts before us are *prescriptive*, which is to say that they do not provide a description of actual behavior or practices—a glimpse of the community as it really is. Instead, they present the author's *ideal*—that is, what a Christian congregation should look like according to his vision. So listen again to 1 Timothy 2:11–12: "Let a woman learn in silence with full submission. I permit no woman to teach or to have authority over a man; she is to keep silent." This is clearly prescription, and prescriptive material is often the best historical evidence we have that the *opposite* is happening.[11] You don't tell women to shut up unless they are talking. You don't command them not to teach unless they are, in fact, teaching.[12]

In short, you put the grease where the squeak is. First Timothy's long lists of qualifications for church leadership did not materialize in a vacuum![13] Real problems and needs are being addressed here, exacerbated by the inadequacy of current community leadership. Indeed, the letters reflect real concern about "signs of deficiency in intellectual, managerial, and even moral qualities" among early church leaders.[14] They advise, "Do not ordain anyone hastily" (1 Tim. 5:22), probably because mistakes have been made and the community has learned some hard lessons.

Let us turn to two texts—1 Timothy 3:1–16 and 5:17–25— that provide a fascinating glimpse of the early church's struggle with these concerns. They contain long lists that prescribe qualifications for church leaders. This is what these early Christians wanted to see on the curriculum vitae of church leaders. The lists don't tell us much about what these ministerial leaders actually *do*, for they are not job descriptions. Instead, they articulate job *qualifications* that, interestingly, highlight moral values and deportment. They present catalogs of virtues that bear a good bit of resemblance to other virtue catalogs that circulated throughout the Greco-Roman world.

I recommend that you stop at this point and read through these texts, pausing to collect your impressions of them and, if you are engaged in group study, to share these impressions with others. What strikes you most about these texts? What captures your attention? And what questions do they raise for you? Moreover, as odd as these ancient lists of qualifications may seem in some respects, do you discern in them positive—or at least realistic—values that should inform reflection on qualifications for church leadership in our own day? I offer observations below as food for ongoing thought.

THE PUBLIC GAZE

The thing that I find most striking—and most sobering—in these texts is the high visibility of the ecclesial leader. Church leaders have a public persona; the public gaze is upon them. From beginning to end, the texts presume "a posture of being watched,"[15] so much so that even in misconduct church leaders have a public role to play (1 Tim. 5:20). The note of divine judgment in 1 Timothy 5:24–25 suggests that even God is watching! As one commentator has observed, given all this hypervigilance, it is no wonder that Timothy needs a prescription for stomach ailments (5:23)![16]

This brings to mind Kudzu, my favorite comic strip character, who seemed to understand something of this public gaze when he turned to his pastor, the Rev. Will B. Dunn, and said, "Being a minister must be really hard, huh, preacher?! I mean, living for others, leading an exemplary life! That's a lot of responsibility! The pressures must be tremendous! Having to set a good example! . . . People watching, waiting for one false move, one sign of human frailty they can jump on! . . . I don't know how you handle it!" The Rev. Dunn replied, "I stay home a lot."[17] Both Kudzu and 1 Timothy recognize that those in leadership roles attract criticism and gossip, which is perhaps why concern that overseers/bishops be "above reproach" is at the top, and in a sense encapsulates, the list of their qualifications (1 Tim. 3:2). They must pass public scrutiny and measure up to high standards of public esteem, else they be subject to gossip and attack. In fact, the odd references in 1 Timothy 3:6–7 to the possibility that an overseer could become puffed up and fall into "the condemnation of the devil" or that he might not be well thought of by outsiders and fall into "the snare of the devil" could be translated another way. The Greek word *diabolos* ("devil") can also mean "slanderer," and it may well be the condemnation and snare of the malicious gossipmonger that threatens the church leader, and by extension, the church.

While sobering, the texts surely direct our attention to a realistic consideration: church leaders play a public and representative role, and "their visibility can either build or erode confidence in the faith that is in Jesus Christ."[18] Moreover, anything that disgraces the leader also disgraces the church.[19] The church leader's conduct thus should give no opportunity to critics to question the integrity of the church and its faith. Conversely, by embodying the best of recognized virtues, the church leader will deflect criticism (of both himself and the Christian community) and possibly attract people to the faith.

BELIEFS AND BEHAVIOR

High ethical standards are thus crucial to an understanding of what it means to be ordained to church office.[20] From beginning to end, the Pastoral Epistles presume a fundamental connection between beliefs and behavior. Indeed, the conduct of church leaders (their orthopraxy) is regarded as every bit as important as their orthodoxy; it may, in fact, be over the long run that their real character is best shown.[21] Anyone can parrot a creed, but deportment—the conduct of, and connection between, one's public and private life—gives embodied witness to the authenticity of faith.

Given the Pastorals' decided emphasis on high ethical standards, one might conclude that belief takes a backseat to behavior. Indeed, Jouette Bassler acknowledges that the Pastoral Epistles have not been noted for their profound theology. But she also goes on to note that their diverse and often mundane exhortations are in fact theologically grounded: "God, the one God, the living God, desires the salvation of all (1 Tim 2:4, 6; 4:10; 6:13; Titus 2:11). This serves as the warrant for the exhortations to the quiet and dignified behavior that not only deflects suspicion but also elicits the approval of the non-Christian world."[22] Moreover, 1 Timothy's description of the church as the "household of God" and "pillar and bulwark of the truth" (3:15) is situated at the very heart of the letter, along with the fragment of a Christian hymn that delineates core affirmations of Christian faith: "The mystery of our religion is great: He was revealed in flesh, vindicated in spirit, seen by angels, proclaimed among Gentiles, believed in throughout the world, taken up in glory" (3:16). The church is not identified with the truth (note that in the original Greek it is described as *a* pillar, not *the* pillar, of the truth), but the church does support the truth and derives its life from it—that is, from the experience of the living God.[23] Moreover, as Luke Timothy Johnson emphasizes, these verses serve as an important reminder of what church structure is actually for: to reveal the mystery of God's presence in the world.[24] They also set how we act in the context of how God has acted toward us in Christ.[25]

FAMILY CONSIDERATIONS

Family considerations figure prominently in the lists of qualifications for church leaders, and some of them are likely to strike modern readers as antiquated, for they reflect conventions of the ancient patriarchal household and first-century notions of respectable family behaviors. The overseer, for example, is expected to "manage his own household well, keeping his children submissive and respectful in every way" (1 Tim. 3:4), as is the server/deacon (3:12). (Not only would this admonition disqualify many church leaders serving today; it no longer accords with accepted parental wisdom.) Moreover, both the overseer/bishop and server/deacon are to be "married only once" (3:2, 12). Translating more literally in each case, the overseer or server is to be a "one-woman man." The reference has occasioned debate: is polygamy or remarriage in view? Since there is little evidence of polygamy among early Christians, most scholars think the point is that overseers and deacons should not remarry after divorce or the death of a spouse (an honorable convention in the first-century world). Fidelity to one spouse is expected.

An interesting ambiguity appears in the discussion of women connected with servers/deacons. In Greek the word for "woman" (*gynē*) is also the word for "wife." So in 3:11, does the text suggest that *wives of deacons* need to be "serious, not slanderers, but temperate, faithful in all things," or is such behavior impressed instead upon *women who were deacons* in their own right? There may be doubt that women served as deacons in the early church (Phoebe, for example, is identified as such in Rom. 16:1). The question is whether women could have played these roles in the communities to whom the Pastorals were addressed, given their explicit strictures on women's leadership (1 Tim. 2:8–15). (I like to think that the author may have been constrained to mention women deacons, albeit in ambiguous fashion, because they *were* serving in diaconal roles—regrettably, in his view, or perhaps in "silent" ways that did not entail "teaching" or "having authority" over men—but their exercise of leadership could not be hidden![26] It is also worth noting that overseers/bishops and servers/deacons are held to very similar ethical standards, and there is no parallel discussion about the wives of bishops.) In today's mainline Protestant denominations, at least, there is no longer any question that women are eligible for service as bishops, pastors, elders, and deacons.

It perhaps also needs to be said that the Pastoral Epistles do not require that overseers, elders, and servers be married; they simply presume that they are (in contrast to false teachers who would forbid it; 1 Tim. 4:3). So these letters should hardly be cited as grounds for barring single persons from positions of church leadership. After all, the apostle Paul himself, in whose name the letter is written, chose a celibate lifestyle, as did Jesus! In short, in many instances the Pastorals' understanding of what constitutes "sound behavior" is strongly influenced by the conventional wisdom of the Greco-Roman world.[27] There is nothing in the list of qualifications that any good Roman would not recognize as a virtue. Thus, as Raymond Brown suggests, "since sometimes the requirements have to do with public respectability, they can and should change in the course of time," as the conventions of public respectability change.[28] Few denominations today, for example, would hesitate to ordain a remarried widower. Even divorce is no longer the instant disqualifier for ministry that it used to be.

This said, despite antiquated mores, are there not also abiding insights in the Pastorals' treatment of family considerations? Is it not striking, for example, that the family is seen as a primary arena of discipleship, and a pertinent one for the formation and testing of a church leader? And shouldn't church leaders evince some "competency in primary human relationships" among those to whom they are "most constantly and fully accountable"?[29] Indeed, could it even be said, as Thomas Oden does, that "guiding the community of faith is something like parenting an extended family"?[30] Surely these are matters of continuing relevance in the church's ongoing discernment of worthy leaders.

ODDITIES

These ancient lists of qualifications for church leadership may include a number of oddities and surprises for modern readers. Not least among them are the rather obvious observations. Does it really need to be said that an overseer/bishop should not be a drunkard, or a bully itching for a fight? Shouldn't this go without saying? Were they really in need of basic instruction in civility, in the rudiments of civilized behavior? As one commentator observes, it makes one wonder about the pool of candidates lining up for these positions that such instructions were thought to be necessary.[31]

Another surprise may be the frequency with which the texts reference indulgence in wine (1 Tim. 3:3, 8; 5:23). As John Calvin put it, 1 Timothy advises that church leaders avoid "intemperance in guzzling."[32] Timothy, however, seems to need encouragement to guzzle a bit more than he does, given his stomach and frequent ailments (5:23). One gets the sense that he was a stressed-out young man, given the heavy responsibilities upon his shoulders, and in need of wine as a relaxant. Perhaps we should appreciate the author's frank recognition here and elsewhere that ministry is time-consuming, fatiguing work (perhaps especially the ministry of "preaching and teaching," described in 5:17 with the vocabulary of "laboring"— *kopiaō* in Greek, a word connoting demanding effort), and that church leaders may need to be exhorted to attend to their diet and health—to matters of self-care. It is also interesting to observe the author's charting of a middle course between ascetic abstinence and abuse of alcohol. The "false teachers" vilified in the letter appear to have recommended abstinence from certain foods (see 4:3–5), perhaps from wine as well. Apparently, the author feels a need to emphasize that food and wine are in fact good gifts of God's creation when enjoyed in moderation. Perhaps it also needs to be said that virtues such as sobriety and marital fidelity should not be glossed over too quickly as obvious or trivial. As Luke Timothy Johnson points out, for a

majority of persons "these virtues represent a sort of quiet hero-
ism, won day by day."[33] Perhaps we should also appreciate the
clear implication that the grace of God has an educative function, that it shapes us as human social creatures.[34]

But just as surprising as some of the qualities included in the
lists are some that are missing—qualifications for leadership
that we might well have expected to see. The lists are surpris-
ingly short, for example, on explicitly Christian virtues, with
but two exceptions. Servers/deacons are to "hold fast to the
mystery of the faith with a clear conscience"—the most distinc-
tively theological criterion in the lists—so that their service is
clearly and deeply grounded in Christian faith (3:9). And over-
seers/bishops are not to be "recent converts" (3:6), an admonition that employs a wonderfully descriptive word: they are not
to be "newly planted" (*neophyton* in Greek), that is, "seedlings"
still searching for roots. As a seminary professor, I would like to
see some reference to theological education among the lists of
qualifications! But no special training is mentioned that sets the
church leaders apart. Nor is there any discussion of a person's
sense of "call" to church office. First Timothy speaks, instead, of
the role of overseer/bishop at least as one to which people might
(and apparently did) "aspire" (3:1).

We might also have expected to see more charismatic qualities among the list of qualifications for church office. There is
no reference to eloquence in speaking, for example, or to
prophetic passion. Instead, the lists feature quiet virtues, more
pedestrian, institutional qualities[35]: seriousness, sobriety, lack
of greed and competency in financial affairs, irenic demeanor,
moral and familial stability, and managerial prowess. Qualities
such as these facilitate harmony and sustain a community over
the long haul. Given these considerations, questions have been
raised as to whether the apostle Paul himself would have qualified for church office. He was, after all, a recent convert, a
bachelor who managed no household, feisty, and occasionally
quick-tempered and undignified. As Raymond Brown has
observed, "Rough vitality and a willingness to fight bare-

knuckled for the Gospel were part of what made Paul a great missionary, but such characteristics might have made him a poor residential community supervisor." So "fortunately for all, perhaps, Paul's missionary genius kept him on the move."[36]

A DISCIPLINED COMMUNITY

The Pastorals also present us with an image of a church that disciplines itself. Indeed, they reflect a period in which stated procedures for discipline are in an early stage of development. Careful discernment must accompany assumption of church office in the first place. Thus, a period of "testing" is required for service as a deacon (1 Tim. 3:10), and Timothy is advised not to "ordain" or "lay hands" on anyone hastily (5:22). Communities need to make careful choices of persons in offices of leadership. The letters also acknowledge frankly that church leaders have feet of clay, that they can stumble and even "persist in sin" (5:20). (The reference to elders who "rule well" in 5:17 implies, perhaps, that some do not.) However, because church leaders are easily subject to gossip and criticism, they must be protected from false accusations, for they have a right to judicial equity and their good name. Thus, 1 Timothy 5:17–20 insists on just procedures for dealing with accusations.

But failure among persons in positions of church leadership must be dealt with forthrightly. Luke Timothy Johnson articulates three astute propositions, gleaned from the Pastorals' discussion on church discipline, that provide important food for thought on this matter. First, Johnson notes that "if a church is to be a *church* and not a sect, it must have ways of dealing with failure and even sin. . . . A church must find ways to reveal and heal moral sickness within it. It must do this even, or especially, when it is the leadership of the community which is diseased." Second, he observes that "if a church is to live according to the standards of 'impartiality' mandated by Scripture (and the

Lord), then it must have *just procedures* for the resolution of these failures and sins. . . . The church cannot dismiss its leaders on the basis of idiosyncratic complaints or whispering campaigns. Charges must be openly stated and supported, 'by two or thee witnesses.' On the other hand, those who do wrong in positions of leadership cannot be protected and camouflaged, for to do so is to corrupt the church itself." Third, Johnson concludes that "if a church is to continue to be a *community of holiness* and maintain its distinct identity in the world, it must learn itself how to exercise judgment within it. . . . The community has the responsibility for maintaining its own standards." Indeed, he continues, "when wrongdoing or corruption in the community are not dealt with 'by the saints,' then at some point they will be dealt with by referral to outside authorities. When that happens, there is no more community, only a loose assemblage of litigants."[37] Are these not sobering observations that bear on the integrity of the church's witness?

Deborah Krause also provides food for thought when she highlights the continuing relevance in her own denomination of the Pastorals' special emphasis on right behavior and discipline:

> In a sense, concern for "correct behaviour" is still what guides the leadership of the church in its various expressions today. In the life of my own denomination, the Presbyterian Church (U.S.A.), oversight for the behaviour of clergy occupies a great deal of the energy of local presbytery leadership and committees. Clergy misconduct, particularly in areas of sexual and financial issues, sets the agenda for many meetings of the Committee on Ministry of various Presbyteries, which in many ways functions in PC(USA) polity as the local "Bishop."[38]

Christians in other communions will no doubt discern parallels with their own denominational realities, for it is clear that the oversight of the conduct of church leaders is, as Krause puts it, "an ongoing reality and burden for the institutional church."[39]

THE TENSION BETWEEN THE IDEAL
AND THE REAL

First Timothy presents one final point of connection, one final ongoing reality in the life of the church that warrants reflection. As we have seen, the texts in 1 Timothy 3 and 5 are prescriptive (rather than descriptive) and thus present us with the ideal of church leadership. But in so doing they also give us a glimpse of the tension between the ideal and the real. The author surely hopes for a church in which overseers are "above reproach" and elders "rule well," but as Krause perceptively observes, he reckons with "the reality of a church in which charges are being brought against church leaders, public rebukes have been necessary to enforce an atmosphere of accountability and even 'Timothy' needs to be reminded to keep himself pure."[40] The utter realism with which the Pastorals confront such issues ought not to escape us.

The tension between the ideal of church leadership and the reality is worth noting, for it is certainly one with which we continue to live and struggle. Indeed, it may be of some comfort to see the early church wrestling with this tension as well. Candidates presenting themselves for church office today may actually look much more promising once we have considered 1 Timothy and some of the intellectual, managerial, and even moral deficiencies with which early Christian churches were apparently grappling. Indeed, the tension between the ideal and the real reflected in these early Christian texts should check our recurrent tendency to lapse into nostalgia for the "good old days." We continue to promulgate the fallacy that "things just aren't like they used to be," that the problems we deal with are more difficult and more intractable than any the church faced in the past, and that our leadership is much less up to the challenges of ministry.

One of my faculty colleagues, Ken McFayden, has written about this matter in a perceptive essay entitled "The Crisis of Pastoral Leadership: A Vocation in Crisis?"[41] Ken has spent most of his career working with seminarians, pastors, and other church leaders around issues of call, preparation for ministry, vocational satisfaction, leadership effectiveness, conflict management, burnout, and self-care, and in this essay he reflects on the challenge of accurately identifying why we have a leadership crisis in the church. He reviews the variety of proposed reasons for this crisis, the standard laments, which usually go something like this: "There are too many seminarians who never should have been accepted in seminary in the first place." "There are too many pastoral leaders who are neither pastoral nor leaders." "The mainline church has become so marginalized in our culture that it can no longer attract the best and the brightest." "Theological schools do not adequately prepare students for effective ministry in congregations." As Ken notes, we each have our preferred lament, and "it seemingly has become fashionable to blame our seminarians, our pastors, our churches, and our seminaries. . . . It is easier to blame others and to look for easy answers than explore the ways in which we have contributed to the crisis and to explore its complexity." It is much easier to assign blame and make scapegoats of persons and institutions.

I sit on a seminary admissions committee, and so the version of the lament I hear most frequently is that seminaries are no longer attracting "the best and the brightest" to serve as pastors. The best and the brightest are now gravitating to other professions, such as law or medicine. What struck me in Ken's essay was his observation that there is actually nothing new about this lament. In 1899, William Rainey Harper, the first president of the University of Chicago, observed that significant efforts were needed to attract "the best" to seminary and a profession in ministry, as they tended to pursue professions in law or medicine. As Ken points out, "Some things seemingly never change." He also traces that lament throughout the twentieth century—the lament that pastoral ministry does not attract the best and the brightest, whatever that means and however we measure it. As he observes, "The critique was present during the roaring '20s and through the Great Depression. It was present during the church boom of the 1950s. It was present during the Vietnam War, when a number of young men accepted a call to ministry as a way to avoid a military draft. And it has been there since." "Unfortunately," he continues, "each generation of pastoral leaders, who were told by their predecessors that they were not the best and brightest, have continued to revisit this lament upon younger generations." Indeed, he insists that "we have got to stop using the best and brightest language"—that "there are more effective and constructive ways for us to think about the complexity of the leadership crisis we are facing as a church." Moreover, "this message has got to be hurting pastors (and students) as much as it has others since 1899, including those in your generation and mine." Ken's astute observations, like those of the Pastorals, remind us that we are not the first to wrestle with matters related to church leaders and their qualifications. The tension between the ideal of church leadership and the reality has been one with which the church has had to wrestle since its earliest days. Like Timothy and Titus before us, we too must engage in careful discernment, striving to entrust to worthy leaders the traditions we have received.

QUESTIONS FOR DISCUSSION OR REFLECTION

Begin by reading aloud the catalogs of qualifications for bishops/overseers, deacons/servers, and elders in 1 Timothy 3 and 5. Pause to collect your impressions of these texts and, if you are engaged in group study, to share these impressions with others. What strikes you most about these texts? What captures your attention? What questions do they raise for you?

What would you identify as *repeated* concerns that echo throughout the discussion of qualifications and discipline?

Are there any surprises in the lists of qualifications for church leaders? What things might you have expected to see on these lists that do not appear?

Where do you spot points at which our conventions of public respectability have changed and need to be taken into account?

If you or members of your group are church officers (perhaps deacons, elders, trustees, members of a vestry or church council, clergy, bishops), what do you think of these catalogs as profiles of your own qualifications for church leadership? What connections do you discern between these lists and the service you render on behalf of the church? You may wish to consult your own denomination's stated qualifications for church leaders and see if you spot connections. (Members of the Presbyterian Church (U.S.A.), for example, can consult the *Book of Order*, section G-6.0000, on "The Church and Its Officers.")

The Pastoral Epistles are pervaded by a concern for sound teaching and reliable teachers. Where does this emphasis surface in 1 Timothy 3 and 5? What role does teaching competence play in your own expectations of church leaders?

As odd as these ancient lists of qualifications may seem in some respects, what positive—or at least realistic—values do you discern that should inform reflection on qualifications for church leadership in our own day?

What would you identify as strengths and weaknesses of the Pastoral Epistles' vision of the church and its leadership?

First Timothy 5:17–22 has been called the "Elder's Bill of Rights." What are those rights? What do you think of the process described to protect them?

Revisit Luke Timothy Johnson's propositions on church discipline gleaned from his reading of the Pastoral Epistles (pp. 93–94) and articulate your reactions to them. What is your perception or experience of the role that discipline has played in the life of your congregation or denomination?

Is your denomination or congregation currently engaged in conflict over qualifications for church office? If so, why?

What does your study of these texts from the Pastoral Epistles contribute to your reflection on this conflict? What connections do you discern between this early church's struggle and your own?

What new insights have emerged from your reflection on these texts that are especially important to you?

7

Farewell Conversations

John 13–17

One of the most unusual features of John's Gospel is that by the end of chapter 12, the public ministry of Jesus is over! Yet the story of his passion, death, and resurrection does not begin until chapter 18. Between these two chapters John shifts into slow motion, pausing so that we may eavesdrop on Jesus' farewell conversations with his disciples at their last supper together on the night before his death. By means of these conversations (13:31–16:33), and of the symbolic act of foot washing (chap. 13) and of prayer (chap. 17), Jesus prepares them for his departure and for life in his absence. When their table talk concludes, they proceed directly to the garden where Jesus will be betrayed and arrested (18:1).

The conversations to which we are privy are thus private and anguished ones between intimate friends who are about to lose the one who is the center of their life together. Commentator Fred Craddock captures the scene in a memorable image, likening the disciples to children playing on the floor, who happen to look up and see their parents putting on coats and hats. Their questions are three (and they have not changed): Where are you going? Can we go? Then who is going to stay with us?[1] These concerns are the focus of John's "Farewell Discourse": "Little children, I am with you only a little longer" (13:33). "Lord, where are you going? . . . Why can I not follow you now?" (13:36–37). "Do not let your hearts be troubled" (14:1). "I will not leave you orphaned" (14:18).

By means of these farewell conversations, John addresses more directly than any other evangelist, and at great length, the first major crisis of the church: the departure of Jesus.[2] Those in possession of "red-letter Bibles" (in which the words of Jesus are printed in red) will notice that there is more red at this point than at any other in the New Testament. Jesus talks non-stop for five chapters. (Recently I heard someone describe Jesus in John this way: "Wordy is the Lamb"—and nowhere more so than in John 13–17.) By listening closely, we too are prepared for continued life in this world in Jesus' absence. We are given to understand how the church exists after Easter. Three central emphases that emerge in these conversations are of critical importance for the life of any church wrestling with discernment and conflict and will be our focus: the promise of the Holy Spirit or Paraclete, a new commandment, and the church's mission in the world.

"I WILL NOT LEAVE YOU ORPHANED": THE PARACLETE

Jesus' announcement of his imminent departure (13:33) leaves his disciples anxious and distressed. The blow of this announcement, however, is softened by extraordinary words of assurance and promise. Chief among them are these: "I will not leave you orphaned" (14:18)—a promise that refers to the coming of the Paraclete, or Holy Spirit. Disciples will not be abandoned or left to fend for themselves. After Jesus' return to God, the Paraclete will be sent in his name and will accompany them in their continued life and mission in this world.

The concept of the Paraclete is John's own and represents the evangelist's reworking and expansion of traditional understandings of the Spirit. By means of it, John speaks of the Spirit more clearly than any other New Testament witness as a *personal* presence—as Raymond Brown describes it, "the ongoing presence of Jesus while he is absent from earth and with the Father in heaven."[3]

Believers experience the personal presence of the Paraclete in various ways. The word itself defies translation, for it bears multiple meanings, including advocate, intercessor, comforter, and proclaimer. The Greek word *paraklētos* refers to one who is "called (*klētos*) alongside (*para*)"—and the Paraclete is called alongside believers in a variety of capacities.

John's teaching about the Paraclete appears in five blocks (14:16–17; 14:25–26; 15:26–27; 16:7–11; and 16:12–15), each of which provides different insights into the Paraclete's role in the lives of believers. The first thing disciples are given to understand is this: "I will ask the Father, and he will give you another Advocate [*paraklētos*], to be with you forever. This is the Spirit of truth, whom the world cannot receive, because it neither sees him nor knows him. You know him, because he abides with you, and he will be in you" (14:16–17). Interestingly, Jesus speaks of God's gift of *another* Paraclete—for Jesus himself was the first. The Spirit will be to the church the helper, comforter, counselor, and companion that Jesus has been. Indeed, nearly everything said about the Paraclete has been said elsewhere in the Gospel about Jesus. Only one difference emerges: the word "forever." Unlike Jesus, the Paraclete/Spirit will not go away but will remain with disciples forever. Jesus, the Word made flesh, lived on this earth in one time and place. The Paraclete dwells within every believer for all times and in all places, and is thus a more intimate and enduring presence.[4]

As the portrait of that enduring presence unfolds in the farewell conversations, the Paraclete's teaching role receives special emphasis: "I have said these things to you while I am still with you. But the Advocate [*paraklētos*], the Holy Spirit, whom the Father will send in my name, will teach you everything, and remind you of all that I have said to you" (14:25–26). Being a Christian requires an exercise in memory, and it is the function of the Paraclete/Spirit to bring to our remembrance the story of God's Word in the world. The Paraclete teaches nothing other than what Jesus taught, and keeps believers grounded in the tradition of the Word. However, the Paraclete is a *living* teacher who unfolds in new circumstances the implications of what Jesus said. The Paraclete "guides" believers "into all the truth," interpreting in relation to each coming generation the contemporary significance of what Jesus has said and done: "I still have many things to say to you, but you cannot bear them now. When the Spirit of truth comes, he will guide you into all the truth; for he will not speak on his own, but will speak whatever he hears, and he will declare to you the things that are to come" (16:12–13). The Paraclete's teaching role in the community of believers is thus both "conserving" and "creative."[5] That teaching role is to pass on the tradition of what Jesus said and did without corruption, yet also to reveal the mind of Christ in new situations.

In this connection, it is perhaps worth noting that congregations and denominations can find themselves wrestling with the tension between that conserving and creative teaching presence as they seek to discern the mind of Christ together. Believers do not always agree on the direction in which the Spirit is leading. Thus, it is important to note, once again, that the gift of the Paraclete/Spirit is a gift to the whole community. When Jesus talks about the gift of the Paraclete/Spirit, all the "you's" are really "y'all's"—they are plural! The Paraclete is not a private possession; it is given to and known in the community. Thus, it is important for believers to stay together in the midst of disagreement as they pursue discernment, because they need each other to discern what God in Christ, through the Spirit, is calling them to be and do. In the midst of communal wrestling with discernment as believers articulate their deepest convictions, they are challenged and corrected, and the Spirit's leading makes itself known.

This communal mode of the Spirit's leading among us is crucial to bear in mind in the midst of ecclesial family feuds, especially at those times when we are mightily tempted to walk away. Barbara G. Wheeler, a keen observer of church conflict, wisely emphasizes this point:

> Why stay together? We need one another, not only because Christ commands us to seek unity and not only because our opponents are good for our spiritual health, keeping us honest, showing us features of the faith that we and our friends may have neglected. We also need each other to seek and find the truth. If we split, either by schism (one side walking out or banishing the other) or by erosion (people drifting away because their consciences have been bound too tightly), we lose our chance to persuade those with whom we share a confession of faith of the truth we believe we've been given the grace to see. We forbear . . . not because the truth doesn't matter, but because it does.[6]

Indeed, God uses our strong convictions for the testing and strengthening of the church.

Finally, the Paraclete/Spirit accompanies believers as they come into conflict with the world—as surely they will, for they can expect the same reception accorded their master (see 15:18–16:4). When they find themselves called upon to defend their faith or to speak truth to those who hold power, the Paraclete/Spirit appears as a witness: "When the Advocate [parakletos] comes, whom I will send to you from the Father, the Spirit of truth who comes from the Father, he will testify on my behalf. You also are to testify because you have been with me from the beginning" (15:26–27). Consequently, the Christian is no doormat—no passive victim—in the face of the world's hatred and persecution. The Paraclete dwells within, giving voice to truth and empowering unwavering witness. Moreover, the Paraclete/Spirit places the world in proper perspective for believers. This seems to be the point of these enigmatic words: "When he comes, he will prove the world wrong about sin and righteousness and judgment" (see 16:7–11). The world judged Jesus guilty of sin and condemned him to death—but it was wrong! The very experience of the Paraclete in believers' lives is a sign to them that Jesus was in fact vindicated, raised by God, with whom he now abides.

In these many ways the Paraclete fulfills the promise of Jesus, who said, "I will not leave you orphaned" (14:18). The Spirit's presence more than makes up for Jesus' absence: "It is to your advantage that I go away, for if I do not go away, the Advocate [*parakletos*] will not come to you; but if I go, I will send him to you" (16:7). After Easter, the Paraclete/Spirit, the living presence of Christ, abides forever with the church, accompanying, guiding, and empowering its continued life and witness in the world. Moreover, that Spirit is not confined to charismatics or apostles, prophets, teachers, or administrators, but is the possession of every believing Christian.[7] No one has second-class status or secondhand faith, for all have direct access to the Paraclete's revelation of God in Christ. The concept of the Paraclete explains a great deal about the Gospel of John's unique theological vision—its radically egalitarian view of the church and its testimony to the fullness of life available now, in the believer's present experience. It is one of John's most profound contributions to Christian thought—one that, as Gail O'Day affirms, summons disciples "to believe in a life shaped not by Jesus' absence, but by the unending presence of God."[8]

"A NEW COMMANDMENT": LOVE ONE ANOTHER

If a first major emphasis of Jesus' farewell conversations is the gift of the Paraclete or Holy Spirit, a second is the one that may be the hardest for us to hear, particularly when we are in the midst of difficult communal discernment: "Love one another." John is distinguished from the other Gospels by an almost total lack of ethical exhortation. Nowhere in John are disciples encouraged to turn the other cheek, walk the other mile, forgive those who trespass against them, give away possessions, or attend to the poor. Only in the farewell conversations does a "commandment" appear, surfacing early and echoing throughout the discourse: "I give you a new commandment, that you love one another. Just as I have loved you, you also should love one another. By this everyone will know that you are my disciples, if you have love for one another" (13:34–35). It is as close as we get to an ethical injunction in John. Mutual love is at the heart of John's vision of the Christian life. In fact, it is the identifying characteristic of the community that continues to exist in the world in Jesus' name. Such love keeps the spirit of Jesus alive in the world and has evangelistic import, for as long as Christian love is in the world, the world is still encountering Jesus.

However, the commandment may initially strike us as odd, on three counts. For one thing, we may wonder in what sense the commandment can be deemed "new," for a love commandment was, and is, also central to Judaism (Lev. 19:18). But for John the commandment is new in one important respect: it takes Jesus as its model, who gave the fullest possible expression to God's own love by giving his own life on the cross. This point emerges clearly when the love commandment is restated in 15:12–13: "This is my commandment, that you love one another as I have loved you. No one has greater love than this, to lay down one's life for one's friends."

A second question may also give us pause: Can love be "commanded"? Not if it were simply a feeling. But the love of which John speaks is more than the warm feeling one has toward another. It is more than that emotion extolled in Hallmark-speak as "the feeling you feel when you feel you're going to feel a feeling you never felt before." Love, in both the Old and New Testaments, is not just something you feel; far more, it is something you do. Love seeks the well-being of others and is expressed in concrete efforts on their behalf. Thus, love can be commanded. Love is something we do, redefined by Jesus' own act of self-giving. Love is something we do, regardless of how we feel; thus, it may come as a relief to know that we don't have to like everybody—we just have to love them. In fact, a wise teacher, Henri Nouwen, observed that "if we wait for a feeling of love before loving, we may never learn to love well. . . . Mostly we *know* what the loving thing to do is.

When we 'do' love, even if others are not able to respond with love, we will discover that our feelings catch up with our acts."[9]

The third peculiarity appears by way of contrast when we recall that the other Gospels exhort disciples to love their neighbors (Mark 12:28–34; Matt. 22:34–40; Luke 10:25–28) and even their enemies (Matt. 5:43–48; Luke 6:27–36). John's Gospel focuses the love commandment on the community of disciples itself. It speaks of in-house love, calling Christians to "love one another." We ought not to assume, however, that this makes John's love commandment easier to follow. Indeed, Gail O'Day wisely cautions against dismissing the ethical serious-ness of this commandment: "The history of the church and of individual communities of faith suggests that to love one another may be the most difficult thing Jesus could have asked. There are many circumstances in which it is easier to love one's enemies than it is to love those with whom one lives, works, and worships day after day."[10]

I remember seeing an article in which a former moderator (the chief presiding officer) of my own denomination talked about his service to the church, and what struck me was that he said he had never received so much hate mail in his life. He quoted from one unsigned letter that read, "Dear sir, I pray to God every day that you will die before you kill the church." And that may be fairly mild rhetoric compared to that to which more recent presiding officers in various denominations have been subjected. You do not have to listen very long to the nature of the rhetoric engulfing many denominations at pres-ent to realize that loving one another may indeed be the very hardest thing that Jesus requires of us. Those who have ever found themselves in the midst of congregational or denomina-tional conflict know how difficult it can be to love fellow believers, for no quarrel is as fierce as a family feud. In the midst of communal conflict, we may find ourselves empathiz-ing with the little girl who was asked by her Sunday school teacher if she wanted to go to heaven. The girl replied, "Not if all these people are going to be there." I take comfort in the fact that Jesus promised that there are many rooms in his Father's house (14:1–4), and I must confess that sometimes I pray, "Please, please, please, Jesus, as you prepare the rooms and make the reservations, don't assign me to a room with . . ." In my own life at least, and perhaps in yours as well, loving other Christians may be the most difficult thing that Jesus asks. But to love Jesus is to be obedient to his commandment—not simply for our own sake but for the sake of the world, as we will see when we consider the third major focus of the farewell conversations.

"THAT THEY MAY ALL BE ONE": CHRISTIAN UNITY

John's vision of the Christian life has profound spiritual depths. But spirituality in John is by no means an otherworldly experience or an end in itself. This Gospel is decidedly world-engaged. Indeed, throughout the farewell conversations, Jesus makes it clear that though he is departing the world, his disciples are staying and have a mission in the world that is a continuation of his own (17:11, 14–15, 18). From John's perspective, the church is decidedly "in the world," but not "of the world" (17:11, 16 RSV), a witness to the possibility of a different way of living that challenges the world's false values. The world lives under an illusion that relationship with God is unnecessary, that human existence is independent of its Creator.[11] Jesus demonstrated the truth about God, revealing the love of a gracious Creator, and upon his departure the community of believers continues to bear that witness.

This point finds clearest expression in Jesus' final prayer (John 17), which brings the farewell conversations to a grand conclusion, for the last thing Jesus does to prepare his disciples for his departure is to pray—the longest prayer of Jesus in any of the Gospels. As we eavesdrop on this prayer we hear Jesus pray first for himself as he comes at last to the hour to which his whole ministry has moved (17:1–5), then for his disciples, that they may be protected and upheld in their mission in the world, which is the continuation of his own (17:6–19). Then finally, he expands the circle of those for whom he prays, including those who will believe through the preaching of those first disciples (17:20–26)—which is to say, he is praying for us, the church of the future. And chief among his petitions in our behalf is his prayer for our unity, that we "may all be one. As you, Father, are in me and I am in you, may they also be in us, so that the world may believe that you have sent me" (17:21). How is the world to know God, to be challenged? Not only through hearing our witness to the gospel, but by seeing and experiencing the embodied witness of a community united in love of one another.

As we overhear Jesus pray, what may we discern about the unity of his followers, lest it slip from our grasp? For one thing, it is clear that God is its source, for it is to God that Jesus prays, and he speaks of the relationship of oneness and love that exists between them—a unity that is foundational to any unity we claim. Jesus opens up his relationship with God to include us. He incorporates all who believe in him into the relationship of oneness and love that he shares with God—a oneness and love that believers make visible and tangible in this world by their unity with each other.

Jesus does not pray that we may all be the *same*, but that we may all be *one*—that we might love one another despite the differences that may divide us. The power of that kind of witness is clearly captured in poet and writer Kathleen Norris's description of her first visit to a monastery. In her book *Amazing Grace*, this is how she articulates her astonishment:

> The person you're quick to label and dismiss as a racist, a homophobe, a queer, an anti-Semite, a misogynist, a bigoted conservative or bleeding-heart liberal is also a person you're committed to live, work, pray, and dine with for the rest of your life. Anyone who knows a monastery well knows that it is no exaggeration to say that you find Al Franken and Rush Limbaugh living next door to each other . . . Barney Frank and Jesse Helms. Not only living together in close quarters, but working, eating, praying, and enjoying (and sometimes enduring) recreation together, every day.[12]

The power of that witness cannot help but claim the attention of our polarized world, for only the divine love could be behind the mystery of it.

It is important for the church to bear this in mind whenever it finds itself in the midst of conflict, for often it is then that the world is watching us most closely, especially when we are engaged in highly publicized debates. To be "one" is not to say that we will be the same, that we will all agree, that there will be no conflict. But as we listen to Jesus pray, we are reminded that the quality of our life together—our ability to make visible the unique relationship that exists by God's grace among us— is our most convincing testimony to the truth and power of the gospel we proclaim.

Moreover, sometimes, in the midst of church conflict, the claim is made that internal discord is diverting believers from the "real" work of ministry, from far more important mission in the world in which they ought to be engaged. However, from John's perspective, the quality of our life together is integral to that larger vocation. Indeed, conflict provides the opportunity to bear witness to the fact that the gospel makes a difference in how we deal with those with whom we disagree— an important witness to make, crucial to our vocation in a world of increasing polarization and violence. Our proclamation is hardly credible without it. As Jesus said, "By this everyone will know that you are my disciples, if you have love for one another" (13:35); and "The glory that you have given me I have given them, so that they may be one, as we are one, I in them and you in me, that they may become completely one, so that the world may know that you have sent me and have loved them even as you have loved me" (17:22–23). It is an astonishing claim: that the "glory" of God, manifest in Jesus, is now transferred to the community of believers! In a very real sense, says Robert Kysar, "the community of believers displays the continuing incarnation" and is now the place where the presence of God is to be found.[13]

For all of these reasons, Jesus' prayer for our unity is the very heart of his prayer on our behalf, and at the heart of our ministry in the world in his name. May it be daily among our prayers as well.

And Lord Jesus, keep praying for us too, that we may all be one, embodying in this world the divine love that is your gift to us, so that the world may know that God sent you.

QUESTIONS FOR DISCUSSION OR REFLECTION

Read aloud the following selections from John's Farewell Discourse: John 13:31–35; 14:15–21, 25–27; 15:12–17, 26–27; 16:7–15; 17:1–26. Following the reading, share briefly: What most captures your attention as you consider these readings? What questions do they raise for you?

Love is not something we feel, but something we do, redefined by Jesus' own act of self-giving. Love seeks the well-being of others and is expressed in concrete efforts on their behalf. Share your reactions to this definition of love.

Share your thoughts about Henri Nouwen's observation on pages 107–108. Have you ever had this experience?

Would you agree with Gail O'Day that it may actually be easier to love our enemies than to love those with whom we live, work, and worship? If so, why is this the case?

When you think about controversial issues that have embroiled your congregation or denomination in recent years, what does it mean to you to love fellow believers with whom you deeply, even passionately, disagree? What might loving one another look like in the midst of church conflicts? Where have you seen such love in evidence? How might you foster it?

Which of John's insights into the Paraclete/Spirit's role in our lives most intrigue you, and why? What is their importance for our understanding and practice of Christian spirituality?

Share your reactions to the Paraclete/Spirit's teaching presence in our midst as both conserving and creative. Can
you think of examples in which you believe that the Holy
Spirit has led the church to embrace new insights in
understanding and implementing Christ's will for the
church?

Has Christian faith brought you or your congregation into
conflict with the world? Why or why not? How has the
Paraclete/Spirit empowered you to defend your faith and
to speak truth to power?

New Testament scholar Raymond E. Brown notes both a
strength and a weakness in John's concept of the Paraclete.
Consider his comment and share your reactions to it:

The thought that there is a living divine teacher in the heart
of each believer—a teacher who is the ongoing presence of
Jesus, preserving what he taught but interpreting it anew in
each generation—is surely one of the greatest contributions
made to Christianity by the Fourth Gospel. But the Jesus
who sends the Paraclete never tells his followers what is to
happen when believers who possess the Paraclete disagree
with each other. The Johannine Epistles [1, 2, and 3 John]
tell us what frequently happens: they break their *koinōnia* or
communion with each other. If the Spirit is the highest and
only authority and if each side appeals to him as support for
its position, it is nigh impossible (particularly in a dualistic
framework where all is either light or darkness) to make
concessions and to work out compromises.[14]

Have you ever had the experience of hearing your name
lifted up in prayer by fellow Christians? How would you
describe your experience of overhearing Jesus pray for us,
the church of the future (17:20–26)?

What does the Gospel of John contribute to your understanding of the church's mission in the world?

In what ways have you or your congregation challenged the
world's false values?

Is the world watching your church at present? What is the nature of the publicity it is receiving? What are the headlines?

As we have seen, Jesus does not pray that we may all be the *same*, but that we may all be *one*—that we might love one another despite the differences that might divide us. Share your reactions to Kathleen Norris's description of the embodiment of this reality in the life of a monastery (p. 110). Is this, or can this be, a reality in your church? Why or why not? What obstacles stand in the way of this?

Jesus' prayer in John 17 suggests that ecumenical commitment is essential to the church's mission. What barriers inhibit our witness to the world that Christ's Spirit makes us one?

How and where have you personally experienced unity with other Christians in local, denominational, or global settings?

What new insights have emerged from your engagement with the farewell conversations and your discussion with each other? What questions linger?

Notes

Introduction

1. John P. Burgess, *Why Scripture Matters: Reading the Bible in a Time of Church Conflict* (Louisville, KY: Westminster John Knox, 1998), xiv–xv.

2. Ibid., xvi.

3. Quoted in Thomas G. Long, "No News Is Bad News," in *What's the Matter with Preaching Today?*, ed. Mike Graves (Louisville, KY: Westminster John Knox, 2004), 147.

4. Raymond E. Brown, *The Churches the Apostles Left Behind* (New York: Paulist Press, 1984), 150.

Chapter 1. Arguing about Scripture

1. *Presbyterian Understanding and Use of Holy Scripture*, A Position Statement Adopted by the 123rd General Assembly (1983) of The Presbyterian Church in the United States.

2. I am indebted to Fred Craddock for this observation and also for the wonderful image of journeying through the New Testament from the familiar landscape of the Gospels through the sometimes difficult turns in Paul and finally down the much less traveled roads near the end of the New Testament. Craddock made this observation and employed this image in a sermon titled "The Sunday I Saw God: Sermon on Revelation 5:1–14," delivered on April 14, 1999, at the Chevis F. Horne Preaching and Worship Conference at the Baptist Theological Seminary in Richmond, Virginia.

3. I am indebted to Robert Kysar for this image. Kysar observes that the Johannine Epistles "take us behind the scenes, as it were, to let us see some of the dirty laundry of early Christianity." See *John, the Maverick Gospel*, 3rd ed. (Louisville, KY: Westminster John Knox, 2007), 169.

4. The word "Johannine" refers to a body of New Testament literature that appears to have emerged out of the same early Christian community

(the "Johannine community") and includes the Gospel of John and the later epistles of 1, 2, and 3 John.

5. Raymond E. Brown, *The Community of the Beloved Disciple: The Life, Loves, and Hates of an Individual Church in New Testament Times* (New York: Paulist Press, 1979), 135.

6. Phyllis Trible, "Wrestling with Scripture," *Biblical Archaeology Review*, March/April 2006, 51. See also Trible, *Texts of Terror: Literary-Feminist Readings of Biblical Narratives* (Philadelphia: Fortress, 1984), 2.

7. The back cover of Brown, *Community of the Beloved Disciple*, bears this description, based on an observation Brown makes on p. 24.

8. The Gospel of John contains three explicit references to expulsion from the synagogue: John 9:22; 12:42; 16:2. The expulsion theory is still a basic working hypothesis in Johannine studies, although important critiques of it have been articulated by Adele Reinhartz and others. See Robert Kysar, "The Expulsion from the Synagogue: The Tale of a Theory," in *Voyages with John: Charting the Fourth Gospel* (Waco, TX: Baylor University Press, 2005), 237–45.

9. C. Clifton Black, "The First, Second, and Third Letters of John," in *The New Interpreter's Bible*, ed. Leander E. Keck, vol. 12 (Nashville: Abingdon, 1998), 406.

10. Brown, *Community of the Beloved Disciple*, 107.

11. Raymond E. Brown, *The Epistles of John*, Anchor Bible (Garden City, NY: Doubleday, 1982), 687.

12. David Rensberger, *The Epistles of John*, Westminster Bible Companion (Louisville, KY: Westminster John Knox, 2001), 113.

13. See Brown, *Community of the Beloved Disciple*, 113–23.

14. This commandment appears in Jesus' Farewell Discourse with his disciples (see John 13:34; 15:12–13).

15. See John 3:16–21; 8:24; 16:9. For a fine discussion of the Gospel of John's distinctive understanding of "sin," see Gail R. O'Day, "The Gospel of John," in *The New Interpreter's Bible*, vol. 9 (Nashville: Abingdon, 1995), 663–65.

16. Brown, *Community of the Beloved Disciple*, 107.

17. For a summary of the task force's conclusions on biblical authority and interpretation referenced here, see *A Season of Discernment: The Final Report of the Theological Task Force on Peace, Unity, and Purity of the Church to the 217th General Assembly (2006)* (Office of the General Assembly [OGA-05–088], Presbyterian Church (U.S.A.)), 16–18. The report is available online at http://www.pcusa.org/peaceunitypurity.

18. Amy-Jill Levine, *The Misunderstood Jew: The Church and the Scandal of the Jewish Jesus* (San Francisco: HarperSanFrancisco, 2006), 205.

19. Black, "First, Second, and Third Letters of John," 427.

20. John P. Burgess, *Why Scripture Matters: Reading the Bible in a Time of Church Conflict* (Louisville, KY: Westminster John Knox, 1998), 130.

21. See Richard B. Hays, *The Moral Vision of the New Testament: A Contemporary Introduction to New Testament Ethics* (San Francisco: HarperSanFrancisco, 1996), 151.

22. This quotation from the Second Helvetic Confession comes from chapter 17, section 5.133 in *The Book of Confessions of the Presbyterian Church (U.S.A.)*. The Second Helvetic Confession was authored by Heinrich Bullinger in 1561 in the setting of Swiss-German Reformed Protestantism.

23. Burgess, *Why Scripture Matters*, 129–30. Burgess references the following sections of Karl Barth, *Church Dogmatics*, ed. G. W. Bromiley and T. F. Torrance (Edinburgh: T. & T. Clark, 1956–1975), IV/1, 451; III/4, 9; and II/2, 717.

24. Burgess, *Why Scripture Matters*, 130. See Dietrich Bonhoeffer, *Life Together*, trans. John W. Doberstein (London: SCM Press, 1954), 90–93.

25. Rensberger, *Epistles of John*, 37.

26. Ibid., 72.

27. Brown, *Community of the Beloved Disciple*, 135.

28. David Rensberger, *1 John, 2 John, 3 John*, Abingdon New Testament Commentaries (Nashville: Abingdon, 1997), 124.

29. Robert McAfee Brown makes this observation in *Reclaiming the Bible: Words for the Nineties* (Louisville, KY: Westminster John Knox, 1994), 25.

30. I am indebted to fellow task force member Barbara G. Wheeler for her clear and insistent articulation of this point.

31. Rensberger, *1 John, 2 John, 3 John*, 155–56; Rensberger, *Epistles of John*, 114–16.

32. Victoria G. Curtiss, "Our Individual Reflections on the Final Report," on *Resource CD: Final Report to the 217th General Assembly (2006) and Additional Materials (Theological Task Force on Peace, Unity, and Purity of the Church)* under "About the Task Force" (Office of the General Assembly, Presbyterian Church (U.S.A.)).

33. My task force colleague Scott D. Anderson used this quotation in a presentation he made to John Knox Presbytery in November 2004 after hearing Marty make this comment on May 11, 2004, during his keynote address at the 2004 National Workshop on Christian Unity in Omaha, Nebraska.

34. Linda Cobb, "Dirty Laundry Reveals Personality Type," http://www.pioneerthinking.com/dirtylaundry.html.

35. J. Clinton McCann, Jr., "Psalms," in *The New Interpreter's Bible*, ed. Leander E. Keck, vol. 4 (Nashville: Abingdon, 1996), 888.

36. James L. Mays, *Psalms*, Interpretation: A Biblical Commentary for Teaching and Preaching (Louisville, KY: John Knox, 1994), 200–202.

Chapter 2. Stepping Out of the Boat in the Midst of a Storm

The following reading of a biblical text also tells the story of the journey of twenty Presbyterians who were entrusted with the task of leading the denomination in discernment of its Christian identity. Selected for their diversity, this theological task force was created to look for a different way for the PC(USA) to conduct its common life—to live with its continuing differences more faithfully—and to explore ways for the church to move forward, furthering its peace, unity, and purity. I presented an earlier version of this Bible study at the conclusion of our five-year journey. While the story emerges out of the life of a particular denomination embroiled in conflict and the experience of a particular group of people with this text, I hope that this reading of Matthew 14:22–33 can serve as a resource for reflection for all who find themselves in the midst of storms and serious ecclesial conflict.

1. Thomas G. Long, *Matthew*, Westminster Bible Companion (Louisville, KY: Westminster John Knox, 1997), 166.

2. While most modern translations read "I am he," the Greek words *egō eimi* can also be translated simply and literally as "I am," thereby capturing important Old Testament background music. These are the words YHWH spoke to Moses from the burning bush (Exod. 3:14) and represent a significant affirmation about the identity of Jesus. In Matthew's view, Jesus is the very presence of "God with us" (see Matt. 1:23; 18:20; and 28:20).

3. Barbara Brown Taylor, *The Seeds of Heaven: Sermons on the Gospel of Matthew* (Louisville, KY: Westminster John Knox, 2004), 57.

4. The Greek grammar of this verse (the use of the particle *ei* with the indicative mood) indicates that this is a "first class condition," which conveys the assumption of truth for the sake of argument.

5. This news story was reported in the *Christian Century* (February 17, 1999), 173.

6. Thomas E. Boomershine, *Story Journey: An Invitation to the Gospel as Storytelling* (Nashville: Abingdon, 1988), 93.

7. Ibid., 103.

Chapter 3. Living with Disagreements

1. N. T. Wright, "The Letter to the Romans," in *The New Interpreter's Bible*, ed. Leander E. Keck, vol. 10 (Nashville: Abingdon, 2002), 749.

2. Paul J. Achtemeier, *Romans*, Interpretation (Atlanta: John Knox, 1985), 214.

3. Ibid., 217.

4. Philip F. Esler, *Conflict and Identity in Romans: The Social Setting of Paul's Letter* (Minneapolis: Fortress, 2003), 341, 343.

5. James D. G. Dunn, *The Theology of Paul the Apostle* (Grand Rapids: Eerdmans, 1998), 682.

6. Ibid., 683–84.

7. Wright, "Letter to the Romans," 406.

8. See Mark Reasoner, *The Strong and the Weak: Romans 14:1–15:13 in Context*, Society for New Testament Monograph Series (Cambridge: Cambridge University Press, 1999).

9. Dunn, *Theology of Paul the Apostle*, 681.

10. Robert Jewett, *Romans: A Commentary*, Hermeneia (Minneapolis: Fortress, 2007), 840–41.

11. Dunn, *Theology of Paul the Apostle*, 686.

12. Luke Timothy Johnson, *Reading Romans: A Literary and Theological Commentary* (New York: Crossroad, 1997), 199.

13. A. Katherine Grieb, *The Story of Romans: A Narrative Defense of God's Righteousness* (Louisville, KY: Westminster John Knox, 2002), 128.

14. Robert Jewett, "Romans," in *The Cambridge Companion to St. Paul*, ed. James D. G. Dunn (Cambridge: Cambridge University Press, 2003), 103.

15. Leander E. Keck, *Romans*, Abingdon New Testament Commentaries (Nashville: Abingdon, 2005), 341.

16. Dunn, *Theology of Paul the Apostle*, 688.

17. Wright, "Letter to the Romans," 733.

18. Grieb, *Story of Romans*, 129.

19. Tom (N. T.) Wright, *Paul for Everyone: Romans*, part 2 (London: SPCK; Louisville, KY: Westminster John Knox, 2004), 98.

20. Ibid.

21. Wright, "Letter to the Romans," 741.

22. See Dietrich Bonhoeffer, *Life Together*, trans. John W. Doberstein (London: SCM Press, 1954), 90–93.

23. Keck, *Romans*, 349.

24. Ibid., 350.

25. Brendan Byrne, SJ, *Romans*, Sacra Pagina (Collegeville, MN: Liturgical Press, 1996), 406.

26. Keck, *Romans*, 344.

27. Ibid., 347.

28. Ibid., 348.

29. Jewett, "Romans," 103–4.

30. Richard B. Hays, "Whether We Live or Die, We Are the Lord's," in *The Art of Reading Scripture*, ed. Ellen F. Davis and Richard B. Hays (Grand Rapids: Eerdmans, 2003), 319.

31. Ibid., 322.

32. David L. Bartlett, *Romans*, Westminster Bible Companion (Louisville, KY: Westminster John Knox, 1995), 129.

33. Ps. 18:49; Deut. 32:43; Ps. 117:1; Isa. 11:10.

34. Achtemeier, *Romans*, 221, 225.

35. Wright, "Letter to the Romans," 739.

36. Jewett, "Romans," 104.

37. James D. G. Dunn, *Romans*, Word Biblical Commentary (Dallas: Word, 1988), 799.

38. Ibid., 814.

39. Hays, "Whether We Live or Die," 322.

40. Wright, "Letter to the Romans," 750.

41. Ibid., 749.

42. Bonhoeffer, *Life Together*, 91–92.

43. Johnson, *Reading Romans*, 198.

44. Hays, "Whether We Live or Die," 319.

Chapter 4. Testing the Spirits I

1. Walter Brueggemann, *A Commentary on Jeremiah: Exile and Home-coming* (Grand Rapids: Eerdmans, 1998), 247.

2. Margaret Odell, "Prophet," in *The Westminster Theological Word-book of the Bible*, ed. Donald E. Gowan (Louisville, KY: Westminster John Knox, 2003), 409.

3. Brueggemann, *Commentary on Jeremiah*, 240–41.

4. Ibid., 243.

5. Patrick D. Miller, "Jeremiah," in *The New Interpreter's Bible*, ed. Leander E. Keck, vol. 6 (Nashville: Abingdon, 2001), 782–83.

6. Brueggemann, *Commentary on Jeremiah*, 249.

7. Robert P. Carroll, *Jeremiah*, Old Testament Library (Philadelphia: Westminster; London: SCM Press, 1986), 537.

8. Brueggemann, *Commentary on Jeremiah*, 252–53.

9. Louis Stulman, *Jeremiah*, Abingdon Old Testament Commentaries (Nashville: Abingdon, 2005), 255.

10. Terrence E. Fretheim, *Jeremiah*, Smyth & Helwys Bible Commentary (Macon, GA: Smyth & Helwys, 2002), 391.

11. Thomas W. Overholt, "Jeremiah 27–29: The Question of False Prophecy," *Journal of the American Academy of Religion* 35 (1967): 245.

12. Carroll, *Jeremiah*, 543.

13. Overholt, "Jeremiah 27–29," 244.

14. Stulman, *Jeremiah*, 248.

15. Carol M. Bechtel, *Life after Grace: Daily Reflections on the Bible* (Louisville, KY: Westminster John Knox, 2003), 61–62.

16. I want to thank my irrepressible colleague Joe Coalter for this astute observation.

17. Miller, "Jeremiah," 788.

18. Overholt, "Jeremiah 27–29," 245.

19. Stulman, *Jeremiah*, 246.

20. Overholt, "Jeremiah 27–29," 249.

21. Miller, "Jeremiah," 787.

22. Brueggemann, *Commentary on Jeremiah*, 232.

23. Fretheim, *Jeremiah*, 397.

24. Brueggemann, *Commentary on Jeremiah*, 247.

25. John M. Bracke, *Jeremiah 1–29*, Westminster Bible Companion (Louisville, KY: Westminster John Knox, 2000), 219–20; italics mine.

26. Fretheim, *Jeremiah*, 397.

27. Miller, "Jeremiah," 783.

Chapter 5. Testing the Spirits II

1. Gordon Fee, *Gospel and Spirit: Issues in New Testament Hermeneutics* (Peabody, MA: Hendrickson, 1991), 111–16.

2. James D. G. Dunn, "Discernment of Spirits—A Neglected Gift," in *Witness to the Spirit: Essays on Revelation, Spirit, Redemption*, ed. Wilfrid Harrington (Dublin: Koinonia Press, 1979), 87.

3. Ibid., 82.

4. J. Paul Sampley, "The First Letter to the Corinthians," in *The New Interpreter's Bible*, ed. Leander E. Keck, vol. 10 (Nashville: Abingdon, 2002), 960.

5. See David E. Garland, *1 Corinthians*, Baker Exegetical Commentary on the New Testament (Grand Rapids: Baker Academic, 2003), 582, 632; Raymond F. Collins, *1 Corinthians*, Sacra Pagina (Collegeville, MN: Liturgical Press, 1999), 491. Some scholars limit prophecy to spontaneous utterance, but as Garland observes, "The moment of revelation should not be restricted to flashes that come only during worship. Revelation can come at other times, allowing the individual to ponder it and share it later, in the next worship" (633).

6. See Dunn, "Discernment of Spirits," 83–87; Dunn, *The Theology of Paul the Apostle* (Grand Rapids: Eerdmans, 1998), 594–98; and Dunn, *Jesus and the Spirit: A Study of the Religious and Charismatic Experience of Jesus and the First Christians as Reflected in the New Testament* (Grand Rapids: Eerdmans, 1997), chap. 9.

7. See Garland, *1 Corinthians*, 567–72.

8. See, e.g., Richard B. Hays, *First Corinthians,* Interpretation (Louisville, KY: John Knox, 1997), 209.

9. Sampley, "First Letter to the Corinthians," 941.

10. Hays, *First Corinthians*, 209.

11. Ibid., 218.

12. Dunn, *Jesus and the Spirit*, 293.

13. Mark Allan Powell, *God with Us: A Pastoral Theology of Matthew* (Minneapolis: Fortress, 1995), 84.

14. Frederick Dale Bruner, *A Theology of the Holy Spirit: The Pentecostal Experience and the New Testament Witness* (Grand Rapids: Eerdmans, 1970), 295.

15. Dunn, *Jesus and the Spirit,* 295.

16. Powell, *God with Us,* 84–86.

17. Bruner, *Theology of the Holy Spirit,* 298.

18. Dunn, *Jesus and the Spirit,* 296.

19. Ibid., 297.

20. Bruner, *Theology of the Holy Spirit,* 297.

21. Ibid., 301. Of course, it could be argued that women are excluded from conversation in 1 Cor. 14:34–36. However, in 1 Cor. 11:2–16 Paul presupposes that women do in fact pray and prophesy in the Christian assembly (though he insists that they must do so with their heads covered). Attention to these much-disputed verses is beyond the purview of

this study. Suffice it to say that many scholars do not believe they represent Paul's own sentiment (and I would concur). Many regard them as an interpolation (a later editorial gloss) or as an articulation of opinions expressed in Corinth (vv. 34–35) to which Paul objects (vv. 36–38). For an overview of scholarly debate of these verses, see Hays, *First Corinthians*, 245–48, and Sandra Hack Polaski, *A Feminist Introduction to Paul* (St. Louis: Chalice, 2005).

22. Garland, *1 Corinthians*, 662.

23. Cecil M. Robeck Jr., "Discerning the Spirit in the Life of the Church," in *The Church in the Movement of the Spirit*, ed. William R. Barr and Rena M. Yocom (Grand Rapids: Eerdmans, 1994), 39.

24. Hays, *First Corinthians*, 250.

25. Ibid., 233.

26. Sampley, "First Letter to the Corinthians," 957.

27. Hendrikus Berkhof, *The Doctrine of the Holy Spirit* (Richmond: John Knox, 1964), 91.

28. Bruner, *Theology of the Holy Spirit*, 297n17.

29. Hays, *First Corinthians*, 232.

30. Sampley, "First Letter to the Corinthians," 957.

Chapter 6. Conflict over Qualifications for Church Leadership

1. Thomas C. Oden, *First and Second Timothy and Titus*, Interpretation (Louisville, KY: John Knox, 1989), 1.

2. Raymond F. Collins, *I & II Timothy and Titus: A Commentary*, New Testament Library (Louisville, KY: Westminster John Knox, 2002), 13.

3. Frances Young, *The Theology of the Pastoral Letters*, New Testament Theology (Cambridge: Cambridge University Press, 1994), 103.

4. Collins, *I & II Timothy and Titus*, 79.

5. Oden, *First and Second Timothy*, 141.

6. Jouette M. Bassler, *1 Timothy, 2 Timothy, Titus*, Abingdon New Testament Commentaries (Nashville: Abingdon, 1996), 69.

7. Elsa Tamez, *Struggles for Power in Early Christianity: A Study of the First Letter to Timothy* (Maryknoll, NY: Orbis, 2007), xxii.

8. Luke Timothy Johnson, *1 Timothy, 2 Timothy, Titus*, Knox Preaching Guides (Atlanta: John Knox, 1987), 75.

9. Lewis R. Donelson, *Colossians, Ephesians, 1 and 2 Timothy, and Titus*, Westminster Bible Companion (Louisville, KY: Westminster John Knox, 1996), 118.

10. Elisabeth Schüssler Fiorenza, *In Memory of Her: A Feminist Theological Reconstruction of Christian Origins* (New York: Crossroad, 1983), 310.

11. Joanna Dewey, "I Timothy," in *Women's Bible Commentary*, ed. Carol A. Newsom and Sharon H. Ringe (Louisville, KY: Westminster John Knox, 1992), 353.

12. See Deborah Krause's helpful discussion of this point in *1 Timothy*, Readings: A New Biblical Commentary (London: T. & T. Clark, 2004), 9–15.

13. Johnson, *1 Timothy, 2 Timothy, Titus,* 76.

14. Ibid., 75.

15. Krause, *1 Timothy,* 68.

16. Ibid., 114.

17. This cartoon appeared in the comic strip *Kudzu* by the late Doug Marlette.

18. Krause, *1 Timothy,* 68.

19. Bassler, *1 Timothy, 2 Timothy, Titus,* 69.

20. Donelson, *Colossians, Ephesians, 1 and 2 Timothy, and Titus,* 119.

21. Johnson, *1 Timothy, 2 Timothy, Titus,* 101.

22. Bassler, *1 Timothy, 2 Timothy, Titus,* 31–32.

23. Johnson, *1 Timothy, 2 Timothy, Titus,* 80.

24. Ibid.

25. Oden, *First and Second Timothy,* 44.

26. Tamez, *Struggles for Power in Early Christianity,* 109.

27. Bassler, *1 Timothy, 2 Timothy, Titus,* 34.

28. Raymond E. Brown, *The Churches the Apostles Left Behind* (New York: Paulist Press, 1984), 36.

29. Oden, *First and Second Timothy,* 142.

30. Ibid.

31. James D. G. Dunn, "1 and 2 Timothy," in *The New Interpreter's Bible*, ed. Leander E. Keck, vol. 11 (Nashville: Abingdon, 2000), 807.

32. John Calvin, *Commentaries*, vol. 21, trans. William Pringle (Grand Rapids: Baker Book House, 1981), 80.

33. Johnson, *1 Timothy, 2 Timothy, Titus,* 81.

34. Luke Timothy Johnson, *The Writings of the New Testament: An Interpretation* (Philadelphia: Fortress, 1986), 405.

35. Brown, *Churches the Apostles Left Behind,* 34–36.

36. Ibid., 35.

37. Johnson, *1 Timothy, 2 Timothy, Titus,* 101–2.

38. Krause, *1 Timothy,* 75–76.

39. Ibid., 76.

40. Ibid., 112.

41. Kenneth J. McFayden, "The Crisis of Pastoral Leadership: A Vocation in Crisis?" in *As I See It Today,* published by Union Theological Seminary and Presbyterian School of Christian Education, Richmond, Virginia.

Chapter 7. Farewell Conversations

1. Fred B. Craddock, *John,* John Knox Preaching Guides (Atlanta: John Knox, 1982), 98.

2. Ibid., 97.

3. Raymond E. Brown, *The Churches the Apostles Left Behind* (New York: Paulist Press, 1984), 106.

4. Ibid., 107.

5. Gail R. O'Day, "The Gospel of John," in *The New Interpreter's Bible,* ed. Leander E. Keck, vol. 9 (Nashville: Abingdon, 1995), 777.

6. Barbara G. Wheeler, from an oral presentation, used by permission.

7. Raymond E. Brown, "Diverse Views of the Spirit in the New Testament," *Worship* 57 (May 1983): 233.

8. O'Day, "Gospel of John," 754.

9. Henri J. M. Nouwen, *Bread for the Journey: A Daybook of Wisdom and Faith* (San Francisco: HarperSanFrancisco, 1997), June 16.

10. Gail R. O'Day, "John," in *The Women's Bible Commentary,* ed. Carol Newsom and Sharon Ringe (Louisville, KY: Westminster/John Knox, 1992), 302.

11. For a clear explication of this point, and of John's understanding of the term "world," see Robert Kysar, *John, the Maverick Gospel,* rev. ed. (Louisville, KY: Westminster/John Knox, 1993), 61–65.

12. Kathleen Norris, *Amazing Grace: A Vocabulary of Faith* (New York: Riverhead Books, 1998), 158.

13. Kysar, *John, the Maverick Gospel,* 115.

14. Brown, *The Churches the Apostles Left Behind,* 121–22.

Scripture and Ancient Source Index

Subject Index

Achtemeier, Paul J., 33
antichrist, 2, 12

baptism, ix, 19
Barth, Karl, x, 11, 53, 62
Bassler, Jouette, 84, 88
Bechtel, Carol, 58
Berkhof, Hendrikus, 78
Bible
  arguing about, ix, xii, 1–21
  arguing about, in Jewish
      tradition, 10
  authority of, ix, 3
  and church, ix–x, 1
  and conflict, ix–x, xiv, 1–2, 5,
      11, 59
  and discernment, xii, 53, 60, 62
  as guide, 3
  as "Holy Scripture," 1
  and Holy Spirit, xiv, 1, 53
  interpretation of, 8, 9, 53, 59, 60
  its "re-minding" of us, 44–45
  as living word, 8, 60
  power of the, x, xii, xiv, 9
  reading in the company of those
      with whom we disagree, x,
      xii, 10, 11, 53
  reading Scripture, discipline of,
      ix–x, 10, 60
  as Word of God, x
bishop. See *episkopos*
Black, Clifton, 5
Bonhoeffer, Dietrich, 12, 41, 42,
    48–49

Boomershine, Tom, 32
Bracke, John, 63–64
Brown, Raymond E., x, 3, 5, 8, 90,
    92–93, 103, 113
Brueggemann, Walter, 56, 61–62,
    63
Bruner, Frederick Dale, 73, 76, 78
Burgess, John, ix–x, 11

Calvin, John, 91
caricatures. *See* stereotypes
church
  and Bible, ix–x, 1
  committee meetings, 78
  as community of conversation,
      10, 76–77
  discipline, 93–94
  diversity of, 45–46, 49–50, 110
  images of, 4, 23–24, 26, 85–88
  as Jesus' family, 46, 70
  love as identifying characteristic
      of, 14–15, 73, 107
  mission (*see* church: witness of)
  unity of, 33, 44–45, 109–12
  witness of, 14–15, 16, 24,
      44–45, 46–47, 77, 94, 102,
      105–6, 107, 109–12, 114
church conflict, ix, xiii, 23–24,
    26, 113
  attitudes during, 37–41, 73
  and Bible, ix, x, 1, 11, 53, 59, 72
  contribution to, our own, 19
  over "essentials," xiii, 33, 44,
      48, 50

131

stereotypes, 9, 26, 34–35. *See also* "conservatives"; "liberals"

Stulman, Louis, 61

Tamez, Elsa, 84

Taylor, Barbara Brown, 27

"testing of spirits," xiii, 10, 14, 17, 53–65, 67–79. *See also* discernment

Theological Task Force on Peace, Unity, and Purity of the Church, x–xii, 9, 17, 19, 25–28, 116n17, 118

"things indifferent." *See* church conflict: over "things indifferent"

Timothy (colleague of the apostle Paul), 91

Timothy, First Epistle to. *See* Pastoral Epistles

Timothy, Second Epistle to. *See* Pastoral Epistles

Titus, Epistle to. *See* Pastoral Epistles

Trible, Phyllis, 3

walking on water, 23–32

Wheeler, Barbara G., 105, 117n30

Wright, N. T. (Tom), 33, 36, 40, 45, 46–47, 48, 51

Zedekiah (king of Judah), 54, 57